C-2354

CAREER EXAMINATION SERIES

THIS IS YOUR **PASSBOOK**® FOR ...

PUBLIC HEALTH EDUCATOR I

NLC®

NATIONAL LEARNING CORPORATION®
passbooks.com

PASSBOOK® SERIES

THE *PASSBOOK® SERIES* has been created to prepare applicants and candidates for the ultimate academic battlefield – the examination room.

At some time in our lives, each and every one of us may be required to take an examination – for validation, matriculation, admission, qualification, registration, certification, or licensure.

Based on the assumption that every applicant or candidate has met the basic formal educational standards, has taken the required number of courses, and read the necessary texts, the *PASSBOOK® SERIES* furnishes the one special preparation which may assure passing with confidence, instead of failing with insecurity. Examination questions – together with answers – are furnished as the basic vehicle for study so that the mysteries of the examination and its compounding difficulties may be eliminated or diminished by a sure method.

This book is meant to help you pass your examination provided that you qualify and are serious in your objective.

The entire field is reviewed through the huge store of content information which is succinctly presented through a provocative and challenging approach – the question-and-answer method.

A climate of success is established by furnishing the correct answers at the end of each test.

You soon learn to recognize types of questions, forms of questions, and patterns of questioning. You may even begin to anticipate expected outcomes.

You perceive that many questions are repeated or adapted so that you can gain acute insights, which may enable you to score many sure points.

You learn how to confront new questions, or types of questions, and to attack them confidently and work out the correct answers.

You note objectives and emphases, and recognize pitfalls and dangers, so that you may make positive educational adjustments.

Moreover, you are kept fully informed in relation to new concepts, methods, practices, and directions in the field.

You discover that you arre actually taking the examination all the time: you are preparing for the examination by "taking" an examination, not by reading extraneous and/or supererogatory textbooks.

In short, this PASSBOOK®, used directedly, should be an important factor in helping you to pass your test.

PUBLIC HEALTH EDUCATOR I

DUTIES
Participates in professional health education services for the department of health. Addresses community groups, writes press releases, arranges demonstration programs, and conducts studies of the needs and resources in the development of programs for schools and communities. Performs related work.

SCOPE OF THE WRITTEN TEST
The written test will be designed to test for knowledge, skills, and/or abilities in such areas as:
1. Basic concepts and common practices in the design and implementation of programs for directing or changing the behavior of certain target groups;
2. Behavioral science concepts related to public health education;
3. Techniques of community organization;
4. Organization of in-service training; and
5. Principles and practices of publicity, promotion, and public relations.

HOW TO TAKE A TEST

I. YOU MUST PASS AN EXAMINATION

A. *WHAT EVERY CANDIDATE SHOULD KNOW*

Examination applicants often ask us for help in preparing for the written test. What can I study in advance? What kinds of questions will be asked? How will the test be given? How will the papers be graded?

As an applicant for a civil service examination, you may be wondering about some of these things. Our purpose here is to suggest effective methods of advance study and to describe civil service examinations.

Your chances for success on this examination can be increased if you know how to prepare. Those "pre-examination jitters" can be reduced if you know what to expect. You can even experience an adventure in good citizenship if you know why civil service exams are given.

B. *WHY ARE CIVIL SERVICE EXAMINATIONS GIVEN?*

Civil service examinations are important to you in two ways. As a citizen, you want public jobs filled by employees who know how to do their work. As a job seeker, you want a fair chance to compete for that job on an equal footing with other candidates. The best-known means of accomplishing this two-fold goal is the competitive examination.

Exams are widely publicized throughout the nation. They may be administered for jobs in federal, state, city, municipal, town or village governments or agencies.

Any citizen may apply, with some limitations, such as the age or residence of applicants. Your experience and education may be reviewed to see whether you meet the requirements for the particular examination. When these requirements exist, they are reasonable and applied consistently to all applicants. Thus, a competitive examination may cause you some uneasiness now, but it is your privilege and safeguard.

C. *HOW ARE CIVIL SERVICE EXAMS DEVELOPED?*

Examinations are carefully written by trained technicians who are specialists in the field known as "psychological measurement," in consultation with recognized authorities in the field of work that the test will cover. These experts recommend the subject matter areas or skills to be tested; only those knowledges or skills important to your success on the job are included. The most reliable books and source materials available are used as references. Together, the experts and technicians judge the difficulty level of the questions.

Test technicians know how to phrase questions so that the problem is clearly stated. Their ethics do not permit "trick" or "catch" questions. Questions may have been tried out on sample groups, or subjected to statistical analysis, to determine their usefulness.

Written tests are often used in combination with performance tests, ratings of training and experience, and oral interviews. All of these measures combine to form the best-known means of finding the right person for the right job.

II. HOW TO PASS THE WRITTEN TEST

A. NATURE OF THE EXAMINATION

To prepare intelligently for civil service examinations, you should know how they differ from school examinations you have taken. In school you were assigned certain definite pages to read or subjects to cover. The examination questions were quite detailed and usually emphasized memory. Civil service exams, on the other hand, try to discover your present ability to perform the duties of a position, plus your potentiality to learn these duties. In other words, a civil service exam attempts to predict how successful you will be. Questions cover such a broad area that they cannot be as minute and detailed as school exam questions.

In the public service similar kinds of work, or positions, are grouped together in one "class." This process is known as *position-classification*. All the positions in a class are paid according to the salary range for that class. One class title covers all of these positions, and they are all tested by the same examination.

B. FOUR BASIC STEPS

1) Study the announcement

How, then, can you know what subjects to study? Our best answer is: "Learn as much as possible about the class of positions for which you've applied." The exam will test the knowledge, skills and abilities needed to do the work.

Your most valuable source of information about the position you want is the official exam announcement. This announcement lists the training and experience qualifications. Check these standards and apply only if you come reasonably close to meeting them.

The brief description of the position in the examination announcement offers some clues to the subjects which will be tested. Think about the job itself. Review the duties in your mind. Can you perform them, or are there some in which you are rusty? Fill in the blank spots in your preparation.

Many jurisdictions preview the written test in the exam announcement by including a section called "Knowledge and Abilities Required," "Scope of the Examination," or some similar heading. Here you will find out specifically what fields will be tested.

2) Review your own background

Once you learn in general what the position is all about, and what you need to know to do the work, ask yourself which subjects you already know fairly well and which need improvement. You may wonder whether to concentrate on improving your strong areas or on building some background in your fields of weakness. When the announcement has specified "some knowledge" or "considerable knowledge," or has used adjectives like "beginning principles of…" or "advanced … methods," you can get a clue as to the number and difficulty of questions to be asked in any given field. More questions, and hence broader coverage, would be included for those subjects which are more important in the work. Now weigh your strengths and weaknesses against the job requirements and prepare accordingly.

3) **Determine the level of the position**

Another way to tell how intensively you should prepare is to understand the level of the job for which you are applying. Is it the entering level? In other words, is this the position in which beginners in a field of work are hired? Or is it an intermediate or advanced level? Sometimes this is indicated by such words as "Junior" or "Senior" in the class title. Other jurisdictions use Roman numerals to designate the level – Clerk I, Clerk II, for example. The word "Supervisor" sometimes appears in the title. If the level is not indicated by the title, check the description of duties. Will you be working under very close supervision, or will you have responsibility for independent decisions in this work?

4) **Choose appropriate study materials**

Now that you know the subjects to be examined and the relative amount of each subject to be covered, you can choose suitable study materials. For beginning level jobs, or even advanced ones, if you have a pronounced weakness in some aspect of your training, read a modern, standard textbook in that field. Be sure it is up to date and has general coverage. Such books are normally available at your library, and the librarian will be glad to help you locate one. For entry-level positions, questions of appropriate difficulty are chosen – neither highly advanced questions, nor those too simple. Such questions require careful thought but not advanced training.

If the position for which you are applying is technical or advanced, you will read more advanced, specialized material. If you are already familiar with the basic principles of your field, elementary textbooks would waste your time. Concentrate on advanced textbooks and technical periodicals. Think through the concepts and review difficult problems in your field.

These are all general sources. You can get more ideas on your own initiative, following these leads. For example, training manuals and publications of the government agency which employs workers in your field can be useful, particularly for technical and professional positions. A letter or visit to the government department involved may result in more specific study suggestions, and certainly will provide you with a more definite idea of the exact nature of the position you are seeking.

III. KINDS OF TESTS

Tests are used for purposes other than measuring knowledge and ability to perform specified duties. For some positions, it is equally important to test ability to make adjustments to new situations or to profit from training. In others, basic mental abilities not dependent on information are essential. Questions which test these things may not appear as pertinent to the duties of the position as those which test for knowledge and information. Yet they are often highly important parts of a fair examination. For very general questions, it is almost impossible to help you direct your study efforts. What we can do is to point out some of the more common of these general abilities needed in public service positions and describe some typical questions.

1) General information

Broad, general information has been found useful for predicting job success in some kinds of work. This is tested in a variety of ways, from vocabulary lists to questions about current events. Basic background in some field of work, such as sociology or economics, may be sampled in a group of questions. Often these are principles which have become familiar to most persons through exposure rather than through formal training. It is difficult to advise you how to study for these questions; being alert to the world around you is our best suggestion.

2) Verbal ability

An example of an ability needed in many positions is verbal or language ability. Verbal ability is, in brief, the ability to use and understand words. Vocabulary and grammar tests are typical measures of this ability. Reading comprehension or paragraph interpretation questions are common in many kinds of civil service tests. You are given a paragraph of written material and asked to find its central meaning.

3) Numerical ability

Number skills can be tested by the familiar arithmetic problem, by checking paired lists of numbers to see which are alike and which are different, or by interpreting charts and graphs. In the latter test, a graph may be printed in the test booklet which you are asked to use as the basis for answering questions.

4) Observation

A popular test for law-enforcement positions is the observation test. A picture is shown to you for several minutes, then taken away. Questions about the picture test your ability to observe both details and larger elements.

5) Following directions

In many positions in the public service, the employee must be able to carry out written instructions dependably and accurately. You may be given a chart with several columns, each column listing a variety of information. The questions require you to carry out directions involving the information given in the chart.

6) Skills and aptitudes

Performance tests effectively measure some manual skills and aptitudes. When the skill is one in which you are trained, such as typing or shorthand, you can practice. These tests are often very much like those given in business school or high school courses. For many of the other skills and aptitudes, however, no short-time preparation can be made. Skills and abilities natural to you or that you have developed throughout your lifetime are being tested.

Many of the general questions just described provide all the data needed to answer the questions and ask you to use your reasoning ability to find the answers. Your best preparation for these tests, as well as for tests of facts and ideas, is to be at your physical and mental best. You, no doubt, have your own methods of getting into an exam-taking mood and keeping "in shape." The next section lists some ideas on this subject.

IV. KINDS OF QUESTIONS

Only rarely is the "essay" question, which you answer in narrative form, used in civil service tests. Civil service tests are usually of the short-answer type. Full instructions for answering these questions will be given to you at the examination. But in case this is your first experience with short-answer questions and separate answer sheets, here is what you need to know:

1) Multiple-choice Questions

Most popular of the short-answer questions is the "multiple choice" or "best answer" question. It can be used, for example, to test for factual knowledge, ability to solve problems or judgment in meeting situations found at work.

A multiple-choice question is normally one of three types—

- It can begin with an incomplete statement followed by several possible endings. You are to find the one ending which *best* completes the statement, although some of the others may not be entirely wrong.
- It can also be a complete statement in the form of a question which is answered by choosing one of the statements listed.
- It can be in the form of a problem – again you select the best answer.

Here is an example of a multiple-choice question with a discussion which should give you some clues as to the method for choosing the right answer:

When an employee has a complaint about his assignment, the action which will *best* help him overcome his difficulty is to
- A. discuss his difficulty with his coworkers
- B. take the problem to the head of the organization
- C. take the problem to the person who gave him the assignment
- D. say nothing to anyone about his complaint

In answering this question, you should study each of the choices to find which is best. Consider choice "A" – Certainly an employee may discuss his complaint with fellow employees, but no change or improvement can result, and the complaint remains unresolved. Choice "B" is a poor choice since the head of the organization probably does not know what assignment you have been given, and taking your problem to him is known as "going over the head" of the supervisor. The supervisor, or person who made the assignment, is the person who can clarify it or correct any injustice. Choice "C" is, therefore, correct. To say nothing, as in choice "D," is unwise. Supervisors have and interest in knowing the problems employees are facing, and the employee is seeking a solution to his problem.

2) True/False Questions

The "true/false" or "right/wrong" form of question is sometimes used. Here a complete statement is given. Your job is to decide whether the statement is right or wrong.

SAMPLE: A roaming cell-phone call to a nearby city costs less than a non-roaming call to a distant city.

This statement is wrong, or false, since roaming calls are more expensive.

This is not a complete list of all possible question forms, although most of the others are variations of these common types. You will always get complete directions for answering questions. Be sure you understand *how* to mark your answers – ask questions until you do.

V. RECORDING YOUR ANSWERS

Computer terminals are used more and more today for many different kinds of exams.

For an examination with very few applicants, you may be told to record your answers in the test booklet itself. Separate answer sheets are much more common. If this separate answer sheet is to be scored by machine – and this is often the case – it is highly important that you mark your answers correctly in order to get credit.

An electronic scoring machine is often used in civil service offices because of the speed with which papers can be scored. Machine-scored answer sheets must be marked with a pencil, which will be given to you. This pencil has a high graphite content which responds to the electronic scoring machine. As a matter of fact, stray dots may register as answers, so do not let your pencil rest on the answer sheet while you are pondering the correct answer. Also, if your pencil lead breaks or is otherwise defective, ask for another.

Since the answer sheet will be dropped in a slot in the scoring machine, be careful not to bend the corners or get the paper crumpled.

The answer sheet normally has five vertical columns of numbers, with 30 numbers to a column. These numbers correspond to the question numbers in your test booklet. After each number, going across the page are four or five pairs of dotted lines. These short dotted lines have small letters or numbers above them. The first two pairs may also have a "T" or "F" above the letters. This indicates that the first two pairs only are to be used if the questions are of the true-false type. If the questions are multiple choice, disregard the "T" and "F" and pay attention only to the small letters or numbers.

Answer your questions in the manner of the sample that follows:

    32. The largest city in the United States is
        A. Washington, D.C.
        B. New York City
        C. Chicago
        D. Detroit
        E. San Francisco

1) Choose the answer you think is best. (New York City is the largest, so "B" is correct.)
2) Find the row of dotted lines numbered the same as the question you are answering. (Find row number 32)
3) Find the pair of dotted lines corresponding to the answer. (Find the pair of lines under the mark "B.")
4) Make a solid black mark between the dotted lines.

VI. BEFORE THE TEST

Common sense will help you find procedures to follow to get ready for an examination. Too many of us, however, overlook these sensible measures. Indeed, nervousness and fatigue have been found to be the most serious reasons why applicants fail to do their best on civil service tests. Here is a list of reminders:

- Begin your preparation early – Don't wait until the last minute to go scurrying around for books and materials or to find out what the position is all about.
- Prepare continuously – An hour a night for a week is better than an all-night cram session. This has been definitely established. What is more, a night a week for a month will return better dividends than crowding your study into a shorter period of time.
- Locate the place of the exam – You have been sent a notice telling you when and where to report for the examination. If the location is in a different town or otherwise unfamiliar to you, it would be well to inquire the best route and learn something about the building.
- Relax the night before the test – Allow your mind to rest. Do not study at all that night. Plan some mild recreation or diversion; then go to bed early and get a good night's sleep.
- Get up early enough to make a leisurely trip to the place for the test – This way unforeseen events, traffic snarls, unfamiliar buildings, etc. will not upset you.
- Dress comfortably – A written test is not a fashion show. You will be known by number and not by name, so wear something comfortable.
- Leave excess paraphernalia at home – Shopping bags and odd bundles will get in your way. You need bring only the items mentioned in the official notice you received; usually everything you need is provided. Do not bring reference books to the exam. They will only confuse those last minutes and be taken away from you when in the test room.
- Arrive somewhat ahead of time – If because of transportation schedules you must get there very early, bring a newspaper or magazine to take your mind off yourself while waiting.
- Locate the examination room – When you have found the proper room, you will be directed to the seat or part of the room where you will sit. Sometimes you are given a sheet of instructions to read while you are waiting. Do not fill out any forms until you are told to do so; just read them and be prepared.
- Relax and prepare to listen to the instructions
- If you have any physical problem that may keep you from doing your best, be sure to tell the test administrator. If you are sick or in poor health, you really cannot do your best on the exam. You can come back and take the test some other time.

VII. AT THE TEST

The day of the test is here and you have the test booklet in your hand. The temptation to get going is very strong. Caution! There is more to success than knowing the right answers. You must know how to identify your papers and understand variations in the type of short-answer question used in this particular examination. Follow these suggestions for maximum results from your efforts:

1) Cooperate with the monitor

The test administrator has a duty to create a situation in which you can be as much at ease as possible. He will give instructions, tell you when to begin, check to see that you are marking your answer sheet correctly, and so on. He is not there to guard you, although he will see that your competitors do not take unfair advantage. He wants to help you do your best.

2) Listen to all instructions

Don't jump the gun! Wait until you understand all directions. In most civil service tests you get more time than you need to answer the questions. So don't be in a hurry. Read each word of instructions until you clearly understand the meaning. Study the examples, listen to all announcements and follow directions. Ask questions if you do not understand what to do.

3) Identify your papers

Civil service exams are usually identified by number only. You will be assigned a number; you must not put your name on your test papers. Be sure to copy your number correctly. Since more than one exam may be given, copy your exact examination title.

4) Plan your time

Unless you are told that a test is a "speed" or "rate of work" test, speed itself is usually not important. Time enough to answer all the questions will be provided, but this does not mean that you have all day. An overall time limit has been set. Divide the total time (in minutes) by the number of questions to determine the approximate time you have for each question.

5) Do not linger over difficult questions

If you come across a difficult question, mark it with a paper clip (useful to have along) and come back to it when you have been through the booklet. One caution if you do this – be sure to skip a number on your answer sheet as well. Check often to be sure that you have not lost your place and that you are marking in the row numbered the same as the question you are answering.

6) Read the questions

Be sure you know what the question asks! Many capable people are unsuccessful because they failed to *read* the questions correctly.

7) Answer all questions

Unless you have been instructed that a penalty will be deducted for incorrect answers, it is better to guess than to omit a question.

8) Speed tests

It is often better NOT to guess on speed tests. It has been found that on timed tests people are tempted to spend the last few seconds before time is called in marking answers at random – without even reading them – in the hope of picking up a few extra points. To discourage this practice, the instructions may warn you that your score will be "corrected" for guessing. That is, a penalty will be applied. The incorrect answers will be deducted from the correct ones, or some other penalty formula will be used.

9) Review your answers
If you finish before time is called, go back to the questions you guessed or omitted to give them further thought. Review other answers if you have time.

10) Return your test materials
If you are ready to leave before others have finished or time is called, take ALL your materials to the monitor and leave quietly. Never take any test material with you. The monitor can discover whose papers are not complete, and taking a test booklet may be grounds for disqualification.

VIII. EXAMINATION TECHNIQUES

1) Read the general instructions carefully. These are usually printed on the first page of the exam booklet. As a rule, these instructions refer to the timing of the examination; the fact that you should not start work until the signal and must stop work at a signal, etc. If there are any *special* instructions, such as a choice of questions to be answered, make sure that you note this instruction carefully.

2) When you are ready to start work on the examination, that is as soon as the signal has been given, read the instructions to each question booklet, underline any key words or phrases, such as *least*, *best*, *outline*, *describe* and the like. In this way you will tend to answer as requested rather than discover on reviewing your paper that you *listed without describing*, that you selected the *worst* choice rather than the *best* choice, etc.

3) If the examination is of the objective or multiple-choice type – that is, each question will also give a series of possible answers: A, B, C or D, and you are called upon to select the best answer and write the letter next to that answer on your answer paper – it is advisable to start answering each question in turn. There may be anywhere from 50 to 100 such questions in the three or four hours allotted and you can see how much time would be taken if you read through all the questions before beginning to answer any. Furthermore, if you come across a question or group of questions which you know would be difficult to answer, it would undoubtedly affect your handling of all the other questions.

4) If the examination is of the essay type and contains but a few questions, it is a moot point as to whether you should read all the questions before starting to answer any one. Of course, if you are given a choice – say five out of seven and the like – then it is essential to read all the questions so you can eliminate the two that are most difficult. If, however, you are asked to answer all the questions, there may be danger in trying to answer the easiest one first because you may find that you will spend too much time on it. The best technique is to answer the first question, then proceed to the second, etc.

5) Time your answers. Before the exam begins, write down the time it started, then add the time allowed for the examination and write down the time it must be completed, then divide the time available somewhat as follows:

- If 3-1/2 hours are allowed, that would be 210 minutes. If you have 80 objective-type questions, that would be an average of 2-1/2 minutes per question. Allow yourself no more than 2 minutes per question, or a total of 160 minutes, which will permit about 50 minutes to review.
- If for the time allotment of 210 minutes there are 7 essay questions to answer, that would average about 30 minutes a question. Give yourself only 25 minutes per question so that you have about 35 minutes to review.

6) The most important instruction is to *read each question* and make sure you know what is wanted. The second most important instruction is to *time yourself properly* so that you answer every question. The third most important instruction is to *answer every question*. Guess if you have to but include something for each question. Remember that you will receive no credit for a blank and will probably receive some credit if you write something in answer to an essay question. If you guess a letter – say "B" for a multiple-choice question – you may have guessed right. If you leave a blank as an answer to a multiple-choice question, the examiners may respect your feelings but it will not add a point to your score. Some exams may penalize you for wrong answers, so in such cases *only*, you may not want to guess unless you have some basis for your answer.

7) Suggestions
   a. Objective-type questions
      1. Examine the question booklet for proper sequence of pages and questions
      2. Read all instructions carefully
      3. Skip any question which seems too difficult; return to it after all other questions have been answered
      4. Apportion your time properly; do not spend too much time on any single question or group of questions
      5. Note and underline key words – *all, most, fewest, least, best, worst, same, opposite,* etc.
      6. Pay particular attention to negatives
      7. Note unusual option, e.g., unduly long, short, complex, different or similar in content to the body of the question
      8. Observe the use of "hedging" words – *probably, may, most likely,* etc.
      9. Make sure that your answer is put next to the same number as the question
      10. Do not second-guess unless you have good reason to believe the second answer is definitely more correct
      11. Cross out original answer if you decide another answer is more accurate; do not erase until you are ready to hand your paper in
      12. Answer all questions; guess unless instructed otherwise
      13. Leave time for review

   b. Essay questions
      1. Read each question carefully
      2. Determine exactly what is wanted. Underline key words or phrases.
      3. Decide on outline or paragraph answer

4. Include many different points and elements unless asked to develop any one or two points or elements
5. Show impartiality by giving pros and cons unless directed to select one side only
6. Make and write down any assumptions you find necessary to answer the questions
7. Watch your English, grammar, punctuation and choice of words
8. Time your answers; don't crowd material

8) Answering the essay question

Most essay questions can be answered by framing the specific response around several key words or ideas. Here are a few such key words or ideas:

M's: manpower, materials, methods, money, management
P's: purpose, program, policy, plan, procedure, practice, problems, pitfalls, personnel, public relations
   a. Six basic steps in handling problems:
      1. Preliminary plan and background development
      2. Collect information, data and facts
      3. Analyze and interpret information, data and facts
      4. Analyze and develop solutions as well as make recommendations
      5. Prepare report and sell recommendations
      6. Install recommendations and follow up effectiveness

   b. Pitfalls to avoid
      1. *Taking things for granted* – A statement of the situation does not necessarily imply that each of the elements is necessarily true; for example, a complaint may be invalid and biased so that all that can be taken for granted is that a complaint has been registered
      2. *Considering only one side of a situation* – Wherever possible, indicate several alternatives and then point out the reasons you selected the best one
      3. *Failing to indicate follow up* – Whenever your answer indicates action on your part, make certain that you will take proper follow-up action to see how successful your recommendations, procedures or actions turn out to be
      4. *Taking too long in answering any single question* – Remember to time your answers properly

IX. AFTER THE TEST

Scoring procedures differ in detail among civil service jurisdictions although the general principles are the same. Whether the papers are hand-scored or graded by machine we have described, they are nearly always graded by number. That is, the person who marks the paper knows only the number – never the name – of the applicant. Not until all the papers have been graded will they be matched with names. If other tests, such as training and experience or oral interview ratings have been given, scores will be combined. Different parts of the examination usually have different weights. For example, the written test might count 60 percent of the final grade, and a rating of training and experience 40 percent. In many jurisdictions, veterans will have a certain number of points added to their grades.

After the final grade has been determined, the names are placed in grade order and an eligible list is established. There are various methods for resolving ties between those who get the same final grade – probably the most common is to place first the name of the person whose application was received first. Job offers are made from the eligible list in the order the names appear on it. You will be notified of your grade and your rank as soon as all these computations have been made. This will be done as rapidly as possible.

People who are found to meet the requirements in the announcement are called "eligibles." Their names are put on a list of eligible candidates. An eligible's chances of getting a job depend on how high he stands on this list and how fast agencies are filling jobs from the list.

When a job is to be filled from a list of eligibles, the agency asks for the names of people on the list of eligibles for that job. When the civil service commission receives this request, it sends to the agency the names of the three people highest on this list. Or, if the job to be filled has specialized requirements, the office sends the agency the names of the top three persons who meet these requirements from the general list.

The appointing officer makes a choice from among the three people whose names were sent to him. If the selected person accepts the appointment, the names of the others are put back on the list to be considered for future openings.

That is the rule in hiring from all kinds of eligible lists, whether they are for typist, carpenter, chemist, or something else. For every vacancy, the appointing officer has his choice of any one of the top three eligibles on the list. This explains why the person whose name is on top of the list sometimes does not get an appointment when some of the persons lower on the list do. If the appointing officer chooses the second or third eligible, the No. 1 eligible does not get a job at once, but stays on the list until he is appointed or the list is terminated.

X. HOW TO PASS THE INTERVIEW TEST

The examination for which you applied requires an oral interview test. You have already taken the written test and you are now being called for the interview test – the final part of the formal examination.

You may think that it is not possible to prepare for an interview test and that there are no procedures to follow during an interview. Our purpose is to point out some things you can do in advance that will help you and some good rules to follow and pitfalls to avoid while you are being interviewed.

What is an interview supposed to test?

The written examination is designed to test the technical knowledge and competence of the candidate; the oral is designed to evaluate intangible qualities, not readily measured otherwise, and to establish a list showing the relative fitness of each candidate – as measured against his competitors – for the position sought. Scoring is not on the basis of "right" and "wrong," but on a sliding scale of values ranging from "not passable" to "outstanding." As a matter of fact, it is possible to achieve a relatively low score without a single "incorrect" answer because of evident weakness in the qualities being measured.

Occasionally, an examination may consist entirely of an oral test – either an individual or a group oral. In such cases, information is sought concerning the technical knowledges and abilities of the candidate, since there has been no written examination for this purpose. More commonly, however, an oral test is used to supplement a written examination.

Who conducts interviews?

The composition of oral boards varies among different jurisdictions. In nearly all, a representative of the personnel department serves as chairman. One of the members of the board may be a representative of the department in which the candidate would work. In some cases, "outside experts" are used, and, frequently, a businessman or some other representative of the general public is asked to serve. Labor and management or other special groups may be represented. The aim is to secure the services of experts in the appropriate field.

However the board is composed, it is a good idea (and not at all improper or unethical) to ascertain in advance of the interview who the members are and what groups they represent. When you are introduced to them, you will have some idea of their backgrounds and interests, and at least you will not stutter and stammer over their names.

What should be done before the interview?

While knowledge about the board members is useful and takes some of the surprise element out of the interview, there is other preparation which is more substantive. It *is* possible to prepare for an oral interview – in several ways:

1) Keep a copy of your application and review it carefully before the interview

This may be the only document before the oral board, and the starting point of the interview. Know what education and experience you have listed there, and the sequence and dates of all of it. Sometimes the board will ask you to review the highlights of your experience for them; you should not have to hem and haw doing it.

2) Study the class specification and the examination announcement

Usually, the oral board has one or both of these to guide them. The qualities, characteristics or knowledges required by the position sought are stated in these documents. They offer valuable clues as to the nature of the oral interview. For example, if the job involves supervisory responsibilities, the announcement will usually indicate that knowledge of modern supervisory methods and the qualifications of the candidate as a supervisor will be tested. If so, you can expect such questions, frequently in the form of a hypothetical situation which you are expected to solve. NEVER go into an oral without knowledge of the duties and responsibilities of the job you seek.

3) Think through each qualification required

Try to visualize the kind of questions you would ask if you were a board member. How well could you answer them? Try especially to appraise your own knowledge and background in each area, *measured against the job sought*, and identify any areas in which you are weak. Be critical and realistic – do not flatter yourself.

4) Do some general reading in areas in which you feel you may be weak

For example, if the job involves supervision and your past experience has NOT, some general reading in supervisory methods and practices, particularly in the field of human relations, might be useful. Do NOT study agency procedures or detailed manuals. The oral board will be testing your understanding and capacity, not your memory.

5) Get a good night's sleep and watch your general health and mental attitude

You will want a clear head at the interview. Take care of a cold or any other minor ailment, and of course, no hangovers.

What should be done on the day of the interview?

Now comes the day of the interview itself. Give yourself plenty of time to get there. Plan to arrive somewhat ahead of the scheduled time, particularly if your appointment is in the fore part of the day. If a previous candidate fails to appear, the board might be ready for you a bit early. By early afternoon an oral board is almost invariably behind schedule if there are many candidates, and you may have to wait. Take along a book or magazine to read, or your application to review, but leave any extraneous material in the waiting room when you go in for your interview. In any event, relax and compose yourself.

The matter of dress is important. The board is forming impressions about you – from your experience, your manners, your attitude, and your appearance. Give your personal appearance careful attention. Dress your best, but not your flashiest. Choose conservative, appropriate clothing, and be sure it is immaculate. This is a business interview, and your appearance should indicate that you regard it as such. Besides, being well groomed and properly dressed will help boost your confidence.

Sooner or later, someone will call your name and escort you into the interview room. *This is it.* From here on you are on your own. It is too late for any more preparation. But remember, you asked for this opportunity to prove your fitness, and you are here because your request was granted.

What happens when you go in?

The usual sequence of events will be as follows: The clerk (who is often the board stenographer) will introduce you to the chairman of the oral board, who will introduce you to the other members of the board. Acknowledge the introductions before you sit down. Do not be surprised if you find a microphone facing you or a stenotypist sitting by. Oral interviews are usually recorded in the event of an appeal or other review.

Usually the chairman of the board will open the interview by reviewing the highlights of your education and work experience from your application – primarily for the benefit of the other members of the board, as well as to get the material into the record. Do not interrupt or comment unless there is an error or significant misinterpretation; if that is the case, do not hesitate. But do not quibble about insignificant matters. Also, he will usually ask you some question about your education, experience or your present job – partly to get you to start talking and to establish the interviewing "rapport." He may start the actual questioning, or turn it over to one of the other members. Frequently, each member undertakes the questioning on a particular area, one in which he is perhaps most competent, so you can expect each member to participate in the examination. Because time is limited, you may also expect some rather abrupt switches in the direction the questioning takes, so do not be upset by it. Normally, a board member will not pursue a single line of questioning unless he discovers a particular strength or weakness.

After each member has participated, the chairman will usually ask whether any member has any further questions, then will ask you if you have anything you wish to add. Unless you are expecting this question, it may floor you. Worse, it may start you off on an extended, extemporaneous speech. The board is not usually seeking more information. The question is principally to offer you a last opportunity to present further qualifications or to indicate that you have nothing to add. So, if you feel that a significant qualification or characteristic has been overlooked, it is proper to point it out in a sentence or so. Do not compliment the board on the thoroughness of their examination – they have been sketchy, and you know it. If you wish, merely say, "No thank you, I have nothing further to add." This is a point where you can "talk yourself out" of a good impression or fail to present an important bit of information. Remember, *you close the interview yourself.*

The chairman will then say, "That is all, Mr. _____, thank you." Do not be startled; the interview is over, and quicker than you think. Thank him, gather your belongings and take your leave. Save your sigh of relief for the other side of the door.

How to put your best foot forward
Throughout this entire process, you may feel that the board individually and collectively is trying to pierce your defenses, seek out your hidden weaknesses and embarrass and confuse you. Actually, this is not true. They are obliged to make an appraisal of your qualifications for the job you are seeking, and they want to see you in your best light. Remember, they must interview all candidates and a non-cooperative candidate may become a failure in spite of their best efforts to bring out his qualifications. Here are 15 suggestions that will help you:

1) Be natural – Keep your attitude confident, not cocky
If you are not confident that you can do the job, do not expect the board to be. Do not apologize for your weaknesses, try to bring out your strong points. The board is interested in a positive, not negative, presentation. Cockiness will antagonize any board member and make him wonder if you are covering up a weakness by a false show of strength.

2) Get comfortable, but don't lounge or sprawl
Sit erectly but not stiffly. A careless posture may lead the board to conclude that you are careless in other things, or at least that you are not impressed by the importance of the occasion. Either conclusion is natural, even if incorrect. Do not fuss with your clothing, a pencil or an ashtray. Your hands may occasionally be useful to emphasize a point; do not let them become a point of distraction.

3) Do not wisecrack or make small talk
This is a serious situation, and your attitude should show that you consider it as such. Further, the time of the board is limited – they do not want to waste it, and neither should you.

4) Do not exaggerate your experience or abilities
In the first place, from information in the application or other interviews and sources, the board may know more about you than you think. Secondly, you probably will not get away with it. An experienced board is rather adept at spotting such a situation, so do not take the chance.

5) If you know a board member, do not make a point of it, yet do not hide it

Certainly you are not fooling him, and probably not the other members of the board. Do not try to take advantage of your acquaintanceship – it will probably do you little good.

6) Do not dominate the interview

Let the board do that. They will give you the clues – do not assume that you have to do all the talking. Realize that the board has a number of questions to ask you, and do not try to take up all the interview time by showing off your extensive knowledge of the answer to the first one.

7) Be attentive

You only have 20 minutes or so, and you should keep your attention at its sharpest throughout. When a member is addressing a problem or question to you, give him your undivided attention. Address your reply principally to him, but do not exclude the other board members.

8) Do not interrupt

A board member may be stating a problem for you to analyze. He will ask you a question when the time comes. Let him state the problem, and wait for the question.

9) Make sure you understand the question

Do not try to answer until you are sure what the question is. If it is not clear, restate it in your own words or ask the board member to clarify it for you. However, do not haggle about minor elements.

10) Reply promptly but not hastily

A common entry on oral board rating sheets is "candidate responded readily," or "candidate hesitated in replies." Respond as promptly and quickly as you can, but do not jump to a hasty, ill-considered answer.

11) Do not be peremptory in your answers

A brief answer is proper – but do not fire your answer back. That is a losing game from your point of view. The board member can probably ask questions much faster than you can answer them.

12) Do not try to create the answer you think the board member wants

He is interested in what kind of mind you have and how it works – not in playing games. Furthermore, he can usually spot this practice and will actually grade you down on it.

13) Do not switch sides in your reply merely to agree with a board member

Frequently, a member will take a contrary position merely to draw you out and to see if you are willing and able to defend your point of view. Do not start a debate, yet do not surrender a good position. If a position is worth taking, it is worth defending.

14) Do not be afraid to admit an error in judgment if you are shown to be wrong

 The board knows that you are forced to reply without any opportunity for careful consideration. Your answer may be demonstrably wrong. If so, admit it and get on with the interview.

15) Do not dwell at length on your present job

 The opening question may relate to your present assignment. Answer the question but do not go into an extended discussion. You are being examined for a *new* job, not your present one. As a matter of fact, try to phrase ALL your answers in terms of the job for which you are being examined.

Basis of Rating

 Probably you will forget most of these "do's" and "don'ts" when you walk into the oral interview room. Even remembering them all will not ensure you a passing grade. Perhaps you did not have the qualifications in the first place. But remembering them will help you to put your best foot forward, without treading on the toes of the board members.

 Rumor and popular opinion to the contrary notwithstanding, an oral board wants you to make the best appearance possible. They know you are under pressure – but they also want to see how you respond to it as a guide to what your reaction would be under the pressures of the job you seek. They will be influenced by the degree of poise you display, the personal traits you show and the manner in which you respond.

ABOUT THIS BOOK

 This book contains tests divided into Examination Sections. Go through each test, answering every question in the margin. At the end of each test look at the answer key and check your answers. On the ones you got wrong, look at the right answer choice and learn. Do not fill in the answers first. Do not memorize the questions and answers, but understand the answer and principles involved. On your test, the questions will likely be different from the samples. Questions are changed and new ones added. If you understand these past questions you should have success with any changes that arise. Tests may consist of several types of questions. We have additional books on each subject should more study be advisable or necessary for you. Finally, the more you study, the better prepared you will be. This book is intended to be the last thing you study before you walk into the examination room. Prior study of relevant texts is also recommended. NLC publishes some of these in our Fundamental Series. Knowledge and good sense are important factors in passing your exam. Good luck also helps. So now study this Passbook, absorb the material contained within and take that knowledge into the examination. Then do your best to pass that exam.

———

EXAMINATION SECTION

EXAMINATION SECTION

TEST 1

DIRECTIONS: Each question or incomplete statement is followed by several suggested answers or completions. Select the one that BEST answers the question or completes the statement. *PRINT THE LETTER OF THE CORRECT ANSWER IN THE SPACE AT THE RIGHT.*

1. The one of the following diseases which is the LEADING cause of death in the 10-to-15 year age group is
   A. cancer
   B. tuberculosis
   C. poliomyelitis
   D. diabetes
   E. rheumatic fever

   1.____

2. The one of the following which would MOST likely be a result of untreated syphilis is
   A. paresis
   B. phlebitis
   C. carcinoma
   D. silicosis
   E. angina pectoris

   2.____

3. The one of the following which is MOST likely to be used in establishing a diagnosis of epilepsy is a(n)
   A. electrocardiogram
   B. spinal x-ray
   C. fluoroscopic examination
   D. electroencephalogram
   E. psychometric examination

   3.____

4. The pathology of diabetes involves the FAILURE of the body to produce an adequate supply of
   A. sugar
   B. carbohydrates
   C. insulin
   D. salt
   E. bile

   4.____

5. The one of the following statements that is TRUE about diabetes is that
   A. it can generally be cured if medical orders are followed
   B. it can generally be kept under control but not cured
   C. it is an infectious disease
   D. blindness is an inevitable result of it
   E. controlled diabetes is a progressively disabling disease

   5.____

6. Scurvy is caused by a deficiency of vitamin
   A. A
   B. B
   C. C
   D. E
   E. K

   6.____

7. Vitamin D deficiency is common because
   A. it can only be injected
   B. it is generally associated with poorly tasting foods
   C. only physicians can administer it
   D. it is not found naturally in many foods

   7.____

8. The one of the following vitamins that is used as an aid in coagulating blood is vitamin
   A. A
   B. B
   C. C
   D. E
   E. K

   8.____

9. The one of the following statements that is TRUE of Duchenne muscular dystrophy is that   9.____
   A. it is transmitted to the male children through the mother
   B. the male is the carrier of the disease
   C. the brain is primarily affected because of a lack of blood supply
   D. it is caused by a nutritional deficiency in the antepartum period
   E. only female children are susceptible to the disease

10. If a patient is repeatedly admitted to the hospital because of a series of mishaps in which he has suffered broken bones, the one of the following that is MOST likely to be true is that he is   10.____
   A. a rigid person   B. a diabetic   C. malingering
   D. accident prone   E. psychotic

11. The one of the following groups of illnesses that is known to be caused by bacteria is   11.____
   A. mental diseases   B. acute infectious diseases
   C. nutritional diseases   D. degenerative diseases
   E. cancerous tumors

12. The one of the following with which Hodgkin's Disease is COMMONLY associated is   12.____
   A. neurasthenia   B. meningitis   C. poliomyelitis
   D. cancer   E. tuberculosis

13. The one of the following diseases in which the determination of the sedimentation rate is IMPORTANT for diagnostic purposes is   13.____
   A. rheumatic heart disease   B. congenital heart disease
   C. hypertensive heart disease   D. diabetes
   E. gonorrhea

14. The one of the following disease classifications that would INCLUDE spinal meningitis is   14.____
   A. cancer or tumor   B. nutritional disease
   C. acute infectious disease   D. focal or local infection
   E. acute poisoning or intoxication

15. The one of the following diseases that may cause visual impairment and blindness is   15.____
   A. ringworm   B. osteomyelitis
   C. poliomyelitis   D. gall bladder disease
   E. diabetes

16. The one of the following that is NOT an anesthetic is   16.____
   A. cholesterol   B. nitrous oxide   C. sodium pentothal
   D. procaine   E. ethyl chloride

17. The one of the following that BEST describes the restrictions to be applied to
    Mr. K., a cardiac patient classified, according to the standards of the American
    Heart Association, as functional, Class IVD, is
    A. limited activity
    B. complete bed rest
    C. four hours rest daily
    D. prohibition of stair climbing, alcohol or tobacco
    E. convalescent status

    17.____

18. Over time, geriatrics has become an increasingly important branch of medicine
    CHIEFLY due to
    A. greater specialization within the medical profession
    B. the discovery of penicillin and aureomycin
    C. advances in medical education
    D. increases in hospitalization
    E. the increase in the span of life

    18.____

19. The one of the following which is MOST likely to be an occupational disease is
    A. cancer   B. cerebral hemorrhage
    C. septicemia   D. asthma
    E. nephritis

    19.____

20. The one of the following that is a NUTRITIONAL disease is
    A. tuberculosis   B. scurvy   C. hepatitis
    D. lymphoma   E. scabies

    20.____

21. Morbidity rate refers to the
    A. incidence of an illness
    B. ratio of births to deaths
    C. bacterial count
    D. degree of disability caused by an illness
    E. death rate

    21.____

22. A pediatrician is a doctor who specializes in the treatment of
    A. children   B. foot diseases
    C. disabling illnesses   D. orthopedic diseases
    E. the aged

    22.____

23. A sadistic person is one who
    A. receives gratification through suffering pain
    B. secures a great deal of satisfaction from his own body
    C. receives gratification from inflicting pain on others
    D. turns all feelings towards others back into his own personality
    E. seeks solace through deep mental depression

    23.____

24. The one of the following which is said to be the masculine counterpart of the
    Electra Complex is the _____ complex.
    A. sexual perversion   B. frustration   C. Oedipus
    D. reanimation   E. repression

    24.____

25. The one of the following conditions for which a patient would be admitted to a state mental hospital is
   A. schizophrenia   B. muscular dystrophy
   C. pathological lying   D. congenital syphilis
   E. psychoneurosis

25._____

26. The one of the following statements which BEST describes the difference between a hallucination and a delusion is that
   A. hallucinations occur only at night
   B. delusions occur only with menopause
   C. delusions are primarily provoked by sexual function
   D. a hallucination has a basis in beliefs or ideas
   E. a delusion has a basis in beliefs or ideas

26._____

27. Finger sucking in early childhood has long been a subject of discussion among psychiatrists.
The one of the following statements that is GENERALLY accepted as true is that
   A. finger sucking denotes pending neuroses and the parents need psychiatric consultation
   B. finger sucking is a normal activity of early childhood and should not be interfered with
   C. finger sucking alters the child's facial contours and should be heavily discouraged
   D. finger sucking by a child over nine months old is due to emotional upset and needs treatment
   E. the physician should discuss possible remedial measures such as guards on fingers

27._____

28. The one of the following who is said to be the *Father of Medicine* is
   A. Hippocrates   B. Pasteur   C. Galen
   D. Sydenham   E. Plato

28._____

29. The one of the following who is credited with the improvement of conditions in mental hospitals and the founding of new ones in the United States is
   A. Andrew Jackson   B. Dorothea Dix
   C. William Knowlton   D. Robert Stack
   E. Rene Laennec

29._____

30. The one of the following doctors whose name is COMMONLY associated with much of the early growth and subsequent progress of medical social work is Dr.
   A. Sigmund Freud   B. Richard C. Cabot
   C. Elizabeth Blackwell   D. Carmyn Lombardo
   E. Thomas Parran

30._____

KEY (CORRECT ANSWERS)

1.	A	11.	B	21.	A
2.	A	12.	D	22.	A
3.	D	13.	A	23.	C
4.	C	14.	C	24.	C
5.	B	15.	E	25.	A
6.	C	16.	A	26.	E
7.	D	17.	B	27.	B
8.	E	18.	E	28.	A
9.	A	19.	D	29.	B
10.	D	20.	B	30.	B

EXAMINATION SECTION

TEST 1

DIRECTIONS: Each question or incomplete statement is followed by several suggested answers or completions. Select the one that BEST answers the question or completes the statement. *PRINT THE LETTER OF THE CORRECT ANSWER IN THE SPACE AT THE RIGHT.*

1.   A highly complex compound containing nitrogen essential for building and repairing of body cells and tissue is
   A. carbohydrates   B. fats   C. proteins
   D. vitamins   E. minerals
                            1.____

2.   Which of the following is *generally* considered superior to other sources of basic amino acids?
   A. Fats   B. Green leafy vegetables
   C. Poultry   D. Fruits
   E. Milk, eggs and meat
                            2.____

3.   The building blocks for the manufacture of proteins in the body are
   A. amino acids   B. carbohydrates   C. fats
   D. thyroxin   E. bile
                            3.____

4.   A *more highly* concentrated source of energy than either proteins or carbohydrates is
   A. hemoglobin   B. vitamins   C. sugars
   D. antibodies   E. fats
                            4.____

5.   Two minerals related to the health of the bones are _____ and _____.
   A. calcium; phosphorus   B. copper; zinc
   C. chloride; iodine   D. fluorine; manganese
   E. sodium; iron
                            5.____

6.   A condition in which the blood is deficient in either quality or quantity of red blood cells is
   A. arteriosclerosis   B. goiter   C. schizophrenia
   D. anemia   E. myxedema
                            6.____

7.   The CORRECT percentage of adult body weight in regard to water is most closely
   A. 35%   B. 45%   C. 50%   D. 60%   E. 75%
                            7.____

8.   The ability to do better physical labor may be achieved as a result of eating a breakfast containing both _____ and carbohydrates.
   A. vegetables   B. minerals   C. vitamins
   D. fats   E. fruits
                            8.____

9. The CHIEF reason for obesity is
    A. heredity   B. overeating   C. glandular
    D. psychological   E. eating proteins only

9.____

10. The MOST effective method of determining sensitivity to food allergies is the
    _____ test.
    A. elimination   B. patch   C. skin
    D. Minnesota   E. Salmonellosis

10.____

11. Of the following, the MOST sensible way to approach weight loss is to
    A. cut out breakfast
    B. cut out midday meals
    C. cut out dinner or evening meals
    D. discuss diet or weight-loss options with your physician
    E. drink less water

11.____

12. Control of bodily activities and movements is the responsibility of the
    A. nervous system   B. endocrine system
    C. thyroid gland   D. parathyroid gland
    E. skeletal system

12.____

13. The products of the endocrine glands are called
    A. hormones   B. chromosomes   C. eugenics
    D. pneumococcus   E. toxins

13.____

14. Olfactory cells are important to us in regard to
    A. tasting   B. touching   C. hearing
    D. smelling   E. production

14.____

15. The taste buds are embedded in the
    A. throat   B. tongue
    C. teeth   D. roof of the mouth
    E. esophagus

15.____

16. Excessive amounts of caffeine may result in
    A. indigestion   B. nervousness   C. sleeplessness
    D. irritability   E. all of the above

16.____

17. On a camping trip, the BEST way to purify drinking water is to
    A. boil the water
    B. filter the water
    C. store the water in reservoirs and allow the impurities to settle
    D. chlorinate the water

17.____

18. Trichinosis is a disease that may result from eating insufficiently cooked
    A. veal   B. pork   C. mutton   D. fowl

18.____

19. The normal temperature of the human body is _____ degrees.
    A. 68.0   B. 90.6   C. 98.6   D. 99.4

19.____

20. The BEST treatment for a cold is to   20._____
    A. take a laxative
    B. go to bed
    C. exercise vigorously to work up a sweat
    D. gargle with salt water or mouthwash

21. If sugar is found regularly in the urine, the disease that may be present is   21._____
    A. diabetes   B. anthrax   C. rheumatism   D. beriberi

22. A psychiatrist specializes in the field of   22._____
    A. psychology
    B. infectious diseases
    C. high blood pressure and other circulatory diseases
    D. mental or emotional problems

23. A person with persistent bad breath should   23._____
    A. clean his or her teeth several times daily to kill the odor
    B. have a medical examination to determine the cause
    C. gargle several times daily to kill the odor
    D. chew gum when with other people

24. The BEST way for students to learn about health is by   24._____
    A. listening to their family and friends
    B. personal experience
    C. studying scientific facts
    D. seeking medical information on the internet

25. Sensitivity to proteins contained in pollen, feathers, etc. may be the cause of   25._____
    A. tuberculosis   B. pyorrhea   C. arthritis   D. hay fever

26. Identify the FALSE statement.   26._____
    A. Ability to drive a car is directly related to maturity and judgment.
    B. It is safe for a good swimmer to swim alone in a regular swimming pool.
    C. A pedestrian should walk on the left side of the road so that he will face
       the cars coming from the opposite direction.
    D. Carrying a passenger on a bicycle is not a safe practice.

27. When a person who has been sick is recovering, he or she is said to be   27._____
    A. regenerating   B. anemic   C. convalescing   D. infectious

28. The tuberculin test is helpful in determining which   28._____
    A. people are immune to tuberculosis
    B. people have been infected with tuberculosis germs and need additional tests
    C. people have recovered from tuberculosis
    D. part of the body is infected

29. Of the following, the disease MOST likely to be fatal is
    A. mumps   B. chicken pox
    C. scurvy   D. tetanus (lockjaw)

30. Identify the TRUE statement regarding treatment of a fever by drinking whiskey.   30.____
    A. There is neither harm nor value in this method.
    B. The use of whiskey to treat a fever is standard medical practice.
    C. It is a little-known method but one that is frequently of value.
    D. It is more dangerous than helpful.

31. Food groups and the Food Pyramid are concepts related to   31.____
    A. the cultural significance of popular foods and beverages
    B. the nutritional value of eating different cuisines
    C. healthy eating and nutrition
    D. reducing calories

32. Identify the MOST accurate statement about the effect of alcohol on muscular   32.____
coordination.
    A. An alcoholic drink just before playing a round of golf will increase a
       player's muscular coordination.
    B. The effect of alcohol on muscular coordination depends largely on the
       health of the individual.
    C. An alcoholic drink just before leaving a party will NOT decrease one's
       muscular coordination in driving an automobile.
    D. There is considerable evidence that the use of alcohol affects muscular
       coordination.

33. If an artery in the lower forearm has been cut, the pressure should be applied   33.____
    A. between the cut and the wrist   B. either at the wrist or the elbow
    C. between the cut and the elbow   D. both at the wrist and the elbow

34. Which of the following statements about posture is FALSE?   34.____
    A. Poor posture makes one appear less conspicuous.
    B. Carelessness is the cause of MOST poor posture.
    C. Poor posture increases fatigue.
    D. *Stand tall*, *Walk tall* and *Sit tall* are the chief rules for good posture.

35. Beriberi, rickets, scurvy and pellagra are examples of _____ diseases.   35.____
    A. circulatory   B. nutritional
    C. communicable   D. occupational

36. Which of the following statements about nutrition is FALSE?   36.____
    A. Most leafy vegetables are rich in vitamins and minerals.
    B. There is no harm in drinking orange juice and milk at the same meal.
    C. Eating fish is associated with improved brain function.
    D. Drinking more than six glasses of water daily is fattening.

37. Historically, another term used for poliomyelitis is   37.____
    A. tonsillitis   B. goiter
    C. infantile paralysis   D. spina bifida

38. The mineral needed by red corpuscles in the blood to help them carry oxygen is   38.____

    A. iron   B. calcium   C. fluorine   D. phosphorus

39. Emotional instability in adults is MOST frequently attributed to   39.____
    A. heredity   B. heart conditions
    C. head injuries   D. childhood home life

40. Accidents due to _____ occur MOST often in the home.   40.____
    A. falls
    B. poisoning from drugs and cleansing materials
    C. burns and scalds
    D. gas poisoning

KEY (CORRECT ANSWERS)

1. C	11. D	21. A	31. C
2. E	12. A	22. D	32. D
3. A	13. A	23. B	33. C
4. E	14. D	24. C	34. A
5. A	15. B	25. D	35. B
6. D	16. E	26. B	36. D
7. D	17. A	27. C	37. C
8. D	18. B	28. B	38. A
9. B	19. C	29. D	39. D
10. C	20. B	30. D	40. A

11

TEST 2

DIRECTIONS: Each question or incomplete statement is followed by several suggested answers or completions. Select the one that BEST answers the question or completes the statement. *PRINT THE LETTER OF THE CORRECT ANSWER IN THE SPACE AT THE RIGHT.*

1. Athlete's foot is caused by   1.____
   A. streptococcus   B. oxides   C. bacillus
   D. fungi   E. streptomycin

2. An adult has _____ permanent teeth.   2.____
   A. 26   B. 28   C. 30   D. 32   E. 36

3. Although some digested foods are absorbed by the bloodstream in the   3.____
   stomach, MOST absorption takes place in the
   A. liver   B. pancreas   C. gall bladder
   D. large intestine   E. small intestine

4. The LARGEST gland in the body is said to be the   4.____
   A. liver   B. brain   C. heart
   D. stomach   E. large intestine

5. Jaundice results from   5.____
   A. excessive amounts of bile being produced
   B. a shortage of lymph
   C. bile ducts being blocked
   D. an improper diet
   E. none of the above

6. When the feces is slowed down in its passage through the colon, a condition   6.____
   of _____ is the result.
   A. diarrhea   B. hemorrhoids   C. indigestion
   D. constipation   E. jaundice

7. Most stomach ulcers are caused by   7.____
   A. irregularities in heart beat
   B. varicose veins
   C. rapid peristaltic movement
   D. bacterial infection
   E. preference for spicy or acidic foods

8. Sleeping pills typically contain   8.____
   A. marijuana   B. cocaine   C. antitoxin
   D. agglutinines   E. hypnotics

9. The Schick test was a procedure used to determine if a person was immune to   9.____
   A. diphtheria   B. scarlet fever   C. typhoid fever
   D. tuberculosis   E. none of the above

10. Most vaccines are made up of
   A. botulism
   B. trichinosis
   C. dead or weakened viruses or germs
   D. anthrax
   E. material from chicken eggs

10.____

11. Tuberculosis is caused by a
   A. virus   B. toxin   C. bacteria
   D. genetic defect   E. toxoid

11.____

12. Hydrophobia is a condition that has historically been associated with
   A. abnormal desire for water   B. rabies
   C. abnormal fear of darkness   D. drowning
   E. fear of heights

12.____

13. Poor posture among school-age children is a(n)
   A. orthopedic defect   B. poliomyelitis defect
   C. osteomyelitis defect   D. epidemiologist defect
   E. none of the above

13.____

14. _____ are generally not used for the diagnosis and/or treatment of cancer.
   A. X-rays   B. Radiation   C. Hormones
   D. Anticoagulants   E. Chemotherapy

14.____

15. Hypochondria describes a person who
   A. fears the dark   B. daydreams
   C. imagines illnesses   D. fears water
   E. enjoys burning things

15.____

16. Alcohol is one type of
   A. tranquilizer   B. pep pill   C. depressant
   D. stimulant   E. all of the above

16.____

17. Ophthalmology is the medical field concerned with the
   A. ears   B. nose   C. throat   D. eyes   E. feet

17.____

18. A basal metabolism test is taken to determine if
   A. the heartbeat is normal   B. the thyroid is functioning properly
   C. constipation exists   D. blood pressure is normal
   E. barbiturates exist in the blood

18.____

19. The astigmatism test will determine a person's ability to
   A. see   B. hear   C. write   D. speak   E. reason

19.____

20. A skin specialist may also be called a
   A. chiropodist   B. epidemiologist   C. dermatologist
   D. podiatrist   E. none of the above

20.____

21. An electro-cardiograph   21.____
    A. photographs the kidneys   B. charts heartbeats
    C. records blood pressure   D. records reaction time
    E. photographs the lungs

22. Regular vigorous physical exercise will gradually   22.____
    A. increase the number of body muscles
    B. develop good character traits
    C. develop a heart condition
    D. increase heart efficiency
    E. weaken a person

23. Another name for hernia is   23.____
    A. laceration   B. groin   C. rupture   D. incision

24. All of the following are treatments for sudden onset of kidney stones EXCEPT   24.____
    A. surgery   B. analgesics
    C. Flomax   D. blood thinners

25. _____ is acted upon by bacteria in the mouth to produce acids that dissolve   25.____
    tooth enamel.
    A. Protein   B. Ascorbic acid
    C. Sugar   D. Phosphorus

26. Hemochromatosis is a condition in which excess _____ is stored in the _____.   26.____
    A. iron; liver   B. calcium; kidneys
    C. lymph; pancreas   D. bile; liver

27. An approved first-aid treatment would be to   27.____
    A. remove a foreign body from the ear with a match stick
    B. use a tourniquet to stop bleeding from a minor wound
    C. treat heat exhaustion with drinks that are high in salts or electrolytes
    D. apply absorbent cotton directly to a burn or scald

28. A blood count of a person suspected of having appendicitis reveals that the   28.____
    number of white corpuscles is normal.
    It may be concluded that the person
    A. probably has appendicitis
    B. probably does not have appendicitis
    C. is developing no resistance to fight a possible infection
    D. needs a blood transfusion

29. Artificial respiration is NOT applied for   29.____
    A. drowning   B. gas poisoning
    C. corrosive poisoning   D. electric shock

30. The term "enriched," as used on food labels, generally refers to bread made of white flour to which has been added   30.____
    A. milk, butter or eggs
    B. nutrients like thiamine, niacin and riboflavin
    C. protein, fiber and fat
    D. calcium, vitamin C and sugar

31. Fatigue due to sedentary or mental work is usually BEST relieved at the end of one's working hours by   31.____
    A. several cups of coffee
    B. eight hours of sleep
    C. a tepid shower
    D. recreational activity of a physical type

32. Which statement on alcohol and its uses is FALSE?   32.____
    A. Alcoholic beverages are useful in preventing and curing colds.
    B. Alcohol is to be avoided in the treatment of snake or spider bites.
    C. It is a mistake to take an alcoholic drink before going out in bitter cold weather.
    D. Alcohol has limited use as a medicine.

33. Normally, constipation is BEST avoided through the use or consumption of   33.____
    A. mineral oil   B. yeast
    C. laxatives   D. foods containing fiber

34. Though rare, tuberculosis cases should be considered primarily a result of   34.____
    A. poor nutrition   B. infection
    C. emotional ailment   D. hereditary disease

35. Gonorrhea is frequently a cause of   35.____
    A. stomach ulcers   B. insanity
    C. baldness   D. sterility

36. One purpose of a periodic health examination is the detection of all of the following conditions EXCEPT   36.____
    A. memory loss   B. heart disease
    C. cancer   D. high blood pressure

37. These hormones help to regulate various body functions. _____ is involved when we get excited or angry.   37.____
    A. Thyroxin   B. Adrenalin   C. Insulin   D. Pituitrin

38. To a person driving a car or riding a bicycle, peripheral vision is MOST useful for   38.____
    A. seeing better at night
    B. reading traffic signs more easily
    C. detecting moving objects at the sides
    D. judging more accurately the speed of approaching vehicles

39. Beer, wine and whiskey should be considered   39.____
     A. foods   B. tonics   C. stimulants   D. depressants

40. A good substitute for oranges as a source of vitamin C is/are   40.____
     A. tomatoes   B. beef
     C. cod liver oil   D. whole wheat bread

KEY (CORRECT ANSWERS)

1.	D	11.	C	21.	B	31.	D
2.	D	12.	B	22.	D	32.	A
3.	E	13.	A	23.	C	33.	D
4.	A	14.	D	24.	D	34.	B
5.	C	15.	C	25.	C	35.	D
6.	D	16.	C	26.	A	36.	A
7.	D	17.	D	27.	C	37.	B
8.	E	18.	B	28.	B	38.	C
9.	A	19.	A	29.	C	39.	D
10.	C	20.	C	30.	B	40.	A

TEST 3

DIRECTIONS: Each question or incomplete statement is followed by several suggested answers or completions. Select the one that BEST answers the question or completes the statement. *PRINT THE LETTER OF THE CORRECT ANSWER IN THE SPACE AT THE RIGHT.*

1. Digestion actually begins in the   1.____
    A. mouth   B. pharynx or throat
    C. trachea   D. stomach
    E. small intestine

2. Vomiting is USUALLY an indication that there is also a disturbance in some part   2.____
    of the body other than the
    A. stomach   B. mouth   C. throat
    D. small intestine E. large intestine

3. The normal breathing rate per minute for an adult is about   3.____
    A. 11 to 13   B. 14 to 16   C. 16 to 18
    D. 19 to 21   E. 21 to 23

4. The MOST important to life is   4.____
    A. milk   B. meat   C. vegetables
    D. water   E. fruits

5. Pneumonia causes an inflammation of the   5.____
    A. throat   B. lungs   C. stomach
    D. nose   E. kidneys

6. The circulatory system does NOT involve the body's   6.____
    A. blood   B. heart   C. lymphatic vessels
    D. spinal cord   E. blood vessels

7. To protect the body from infection and disease is the function of   7.____
    A. platelets   B. white blood cells
    C. red blood cells   D. hemoglobin
    E. gamma globulin

8. _____ carry blood away from the heart.   8.____
    A. Venules   B. Veins
    C. Arteries   D. Capillaries
    E. Descending vena cava

9. Defects that a person is born with are called   9.____
    A. endocarditis   B. congenital   C. cardiac
    D. rheumatic   E. mutations

10. The MOST complicated system in the body is the _____ system.   10.____
    A. circulatory   B. respiratory   C. nervous
    D. digestive   E. motor

11. The autonomic nervous system controls   11.____
    A. voluntary muscles   B. smooth muscle
    C. conditioned reflexes   D. sympathetic movements
    E. involuntary muscles

12. *Spastic* is a term generally used in relation to   12.___
    A. nerves   B. muscles   C. emotions
    D. environment   E. thoughts

13. The colored portion of the eye is called the   13.____
    A. cornea   B. pupil   C. iris   D. sclera   E. retina

14. Your _____ is NOT one of your body's weapons against germs.   14.____
    A. skin   B. hairs   C. nose
    D. antibodies   E. phagocytes

15. Dizziness or faintness may be associated with a disturbance of the _____   15.____
    system.
    A. nervous   B. respiratory
    C. circulatory   D. all of the above

16. The LARGEST number of people are accidentally killed when   16.____
    A. swimming   B. driving   C. walking
    D. falling   E. flying

17. The LARGEST number of accidents occur   17.____
    A. at home   B. in the water   C. on the playground
    D. at airports   E. on highways

18. Shock exists because of   18.____
    A. poor circulation of the blood   B. rapid heart beat
    C. nervous tension   D. drop in body temperature
    E. open wound

19. A floor burn would be considered a(n) _____ wound.   19.____
    A. incised   B. abrasion   C. laceration
    D. puncture   E. bruise

20. A doctor uses a sphygmomanometer to test   20.____
    A. reaction time   B. heart beat
    C. pulse rate   D. blood pressure
    E. amount of sugar in urine

21. Stuttering is USUALLY due to
    A. emotional disturbance   B. nervous tension
    C. high blood pressure   D. lack of muscular control
    E. childhood diseases

22. The capacity of the lungs and heart to carry on their tasks during strenuous activity is called
    A. muscle endurance   B. muscle tone
    C. cardiorespiratory endurance   D. respiration

23. A podiatrist is a specialist who treats the
    A. eyes   B. ears   C. feet   D. nose   E. mouth

24. Malignant tumor is associated with
    A. tuberculosis   B. heart disease   C. rabies
    D. moles   E. cancer

25. Skin pores can be found on all of the following EXCEPT
    A. arms   B. legs   C. palms   D. chest   E. feet

26. The chemical salt of _____, when found in drinking water or applied directly to the teeth, seems to help reduce tooth decay.
    A. chlorides   B. fluorides   C. sulphates   D. nitrates

27. When cold air or cold water hits the skin, the body reduces heat loss *principally* by
    A. expanding the pores in the skin
    B. generating more heat in the muscles
    C. reducing the size of the blood vessels in the skin
    D. making the heart beat faster

28. A cup of coffee with sugar but WITHOUT cream contains only
    A. vitamin B   B. calories   C. protein   D. fiber

29. A deficiency of _____ is a cause of night blindness.
    A. iodine   B. protein   C. vitamin A   D. vitamin C

30. MOST authorities believe the usual cause of color blindness is that it
    A. is an inherited characteristic, and so runs in families
    B. may develop from looking at brightly colored lights, especially red ones
    C. is a contagious infection caused by a filterable virus
    D. is caused by an injury to the eyes

31. Active acquired immunity occurs when a person has a disease and then recovers from it.
    This is common for the diseases of _____ and _____.
    A. tuberculosis; malaria   B. measles; chicken pox
    C. colds; pneumonia   D. diabetes; anemia

32. Fatty liver disease is commonly associated with
    A. alcohol consumption
    B. overproduction of bile
    C. a diet high in eggs and yogurt
    D. an imbalance in hormone production

32.____

33. If improperly maintained, forced-air heating systems in the home can cause a person to experience all of the following EXCEPT
    A. runny nose or congestion   B. dry mouth
    C. allergic reaction   D. pink eye

33.____

34. Antitoxin pertains to
    A. immunization
    B. sterilization
    C. germ-killing drugs
    D. determination of susceptibility to a disease

34.____

35. Someone experiencing hookworm was likely exposed through
    A. eating poorly cooked pork
    B. walking barefoot outdoors for prolonged periods
    C. an inadequate diet
    D. poor ventilation in the home

35.____

36. The most common reason a person is overweight is because they
    A. exercise improperly
    B. have inherited a tendency to be overweight
    C. have an underactive thyroid gland
    D. consume a high-calorie diet

36.____

37. A meal that consists of bread, macaroni, rice pudding and cake contains an excess of
    A. protein   B. vitamins
    C. carbohydrates   D. fats

37.____

38. Which statement about sunburn is FALSE?
    A. Sunburn is similar to any other burn and should be treated in the same manner.
    B. If a person who is badly sunburned develops a fever, a doctor should be called.
    C. A severe sunburn may be more serious than other burns of like extent.
    D. There is no danger of getting sunburned on a cloudy day.

38.____

39. Goiter may be caused by a lack of _____ in the diet or drinking water.
    A. iodine   B. chlorine   C. fluorine   D. bromine

29.____

40. It is FALSE that
   A. secondary sex characteristics generally become evident at adolescence
   B. the female reproductive organs which produce eggs are called ovaries
   C. the male reproductive organs which produce sperm are called testes
   D. girls and boys mature on the average at the same age

40._____

KEY (CORRECT ANSWERS)

1.	A	11.	E	21.	A	31.	B
2.	A	12.	B	22.	C	32.	A
3.	C	13.	C	23.	C	33.	D
4.	D	14.	C	24.	E	34.	A
5.	B	15.	D	25.	C	35.	B
6.	D	16.	B	26.	B	36.	D
7.	B	17.	A	27.	C	37.	C
8.	C	18.	A	28.	B	38.	D
9.	B	19.	B	29.	C	39.	A
10.	C	20.	D	30.	A	40.	D

TEST 4

DIRECTIONS: Each question or incomplete statement is followed by several suggested answers or completions. Select the one that BEST answers the question or completes the statement. *PRINT THE LETTER OF THE CORRECT ANSWER IN THE SPACE AT THE RIGHT.*

1. A state health officer is GENERALLY a
   A. specialist   B. physician
   C. health educator   D. member of the bar association
   E. nurse

   1.____

2. The SEVEREST forms of mental illnesses are classified as
   A. neurosis   B. psychosis
   C. sublimations   D. personality disorders
   E. peristalsis

   2.____

3. A public-health campaign educating people about blood pressure and circulatory health would likely include the definition of
   A. lymph nodes
   B. caloric intake
   C. hypertension
   D. red blood cells, white blood cells and platelets
   E. renal failure

   3.____

4. The appendix
   A. aids in elimination   B. aids in respiration
   C. serves no function   D. fights bacteria
   E. aids in digestion

   4.____

5. Diabetes is a disease of the
   A. pancreas   B. kidney   C. spleen
   D. gonads   E. veins

   5.____

6. MOST all children are born
   A. with astigmatism   B. nearsighted   C. farsighted
   D. unable to hear   E. blind

   6.____

7. Alcoholism is considered a
   A. habit   B. disease   C. sickness
   D. pleasure   E. weakness

   7.____

8. Alcohol is absorbed directly from the
   A. small intestine   B. large intestine   C. stomach
   D. gall bladder   E. kidneys

   8.____

9. Anesthetics produce
   A. a feeling of warmth   B. diseases
   C. a loss of pain   D. freedom from diseases
   E. tuberculosis

   9.____

10. The PRIMARY fault of self-prescribed drugs is that they
    A. are too costly   B. do not cure the cause
    C. are hard to get   D. are too slow in acting
    E. weaken the taker

    10.____

11. Disease-producing bacteria form a poison called
    A. pimples   B. toxins   C. inflammation
    D. spores   E. bacilli

    11.____

12. _____ diseases last for a long period of time.
    A. Chronic   B. Cochlea   C. Anaesthetic
    D. Analgesic   E. Acute

    12.____

13. Rocky Mountain spotted fever is spread by
    A. ants   B. dogs   C. feces   D. ticks   E. flies

    13.____

14. Which word is NOT related to the others?
    A. Antitoxins   B. Antibodies   C. Phagocytes
    D. Vaccine   E. Intravenous

    14.____

15. The MOST frequent cause of death is
    A. cancer   B. nephritis   C. tuberculosis
    D. heart disease E. skin disease

    15.____

16. A group of similar cells working together is called a(n)
    A. organ   B. tissue   C. nucleus   D. nerve   E. bine

    16.____

17. The contraction of striated muscle cells is controlled by the
    A. person   B. nerves   C. heart   D. tissues   E. cartilages

    17.____

18. The muscles are fastened to the bones at both ends by
    A. ligament   B. ossification   C. cartilages
    D. tendons   E. coccyx

    18.____

19. The outer layer of the skin is called the
    A. callus   B. dermis   C. papillae
    D. epidermis   E. cuticle

    19.____

20. Human eggs are produced in the
    A. vagina   B. uterus   C. ovaries
    D. fallopian tube E. conceptus

    20.____

21. Heredity plays an important part in the transmission of   21.____
    A. cancer   B. color blindness   C. heart disease
    D. tuberculosis   E. streptococcus

22. Fatigue is produced by accumulations of dioxide and lactic acid in   22.____
    A. the muscle cells   B. lungs   C. respiratory system
    D. nerve cells   E. cardiac muscles

23. _____ is NOT a function of the bones of the body.   23.____
    A. Support   B. Attachment of muscles
    C. Manufacture of blood cells   D. Protection
    E. Weight control

24. A hernia, or rupture, is more common in   24.____
    A. young girls   B. middle-aged women
    C. infants   D. men
    E. older women

25. The body's _____ glands sit atop the kidneys.   25.____
    A. adrenal   B. pituitary   C. thyroid
    D. parathyroid   E. pineal

26. An inflamed area containing pus is called a(n)   26.____
    A. blackhead   B. impetigo   C. pustule
    D. boil   E. fever blister

27. _____ is(are) the MOST important concerning vitamin D.   27.____
    A. Green vegetables   B. Lean meat   C. Sunshine
    D. Butter   E. Fruits

28. To recover from influenza, it is MOST important to   28.____
    A. rest and hydrate   B. move to a dry climate
    C. exercise by taking long walks   D. take antibiotics

29. Cooking vegetables by boiling decreases their nutritional value in respect to   29.____
    A. proteins   B. starch   C. vitamins   D. fats

30. The _____ destroy disease germs by surrounding and devouring them.   30.____
    A. red corpuscles   B. white corpuscles
    C. blood platelets   D. interstitial cells

31. An unconscious person should be given _____ as a first-aid measure.   31.____
    A. water   B. whiskey or brandy
    C. coffee or tea   D. none of these

32. The scientific name for the female reproductive cell is   32.____
    A. sperm   B. ovum   C. gamete   D. embryo

33. Little or no fiber is contained in   33._____
    A. raw fruits   B. whole-grain cereals
    C. sugar and candy   D. vegetables

34. The term *fracture*, as used in first aid, means a(n)   34._____
    A. bone out of joint   B. broken bone
    C. injury to a cartilage   D. severed tendon

35. A disease in which certain body cells seem to *grow wild*, thereby destroying   35._____
the regular cells and tissues, is
    A. leprosy   B. ulcers   C. cancer   D. hernia

36. It is NOT advisable to use cathartics and laxatives regularly because they   36._____
    A. weaken the muscle tone of the intestines
    B. destroy the enzymes of digestion
    C. cause one to lose appetite
    D. cause one to lose weight

37. Diseases that can be transmitted from one person to another by germs are   37._____
    A. infectious   B. hereditary
    C. allergies   D. non-communicable

38. From a health perspective, a campaign emphasizing the benefits of home   38._____
fruit and vegetable gardens should focus primarily on which of the following?
    A. Harvesting techniques and timing for peak fruit ripeness
    B. The importance of properly storing and washing home-grown foods
    C. Amount of money saved on home-grown versus store-bought items
    D. Relationship between vitamin density and quality of soil mixes

39. The soft tissue that underlies the hard outer enamel of a tooth is called   39._____
    A. dentine   B. cement
    C. connective tissue   D. root

40. Which statement on the reliability and accuracy of health advertising over   40._____
the internet and social media is TRUE?
    A. It is very reliable since it is vetted before being broadcast.
    B. It may be considered reliable since doctors often prescribe many of the
       health remedies advertised.
    C. Most of it is reliable and can be believed by the public.
    D. Much of it is of questionable reliability.

41. The *bends* is a(n)   41._____
    A. gymnastic movement
    B. disease of the intestinal tract
    C. disease of divers and caisson workers
    D. ailment due to inhaling dust

5 (#4)

42. A condition that involves curvature of the spine is 42._____
    A. spinal stenosis   B. anemia
    C. rheumatoid arthritis   D. scoliosis

43. All of the following are procedures performed during the annual physical check-up 43._____
    of an overweight 30-year-old male EXCEPT
    A. blood test   B. urine analysis
    C. blood pressure reading   D. prostate exam

44. _____ applies to the destruction of bacteria. 44._____
    A. Quarantine   B. Vaccination   C. Disinfection   D. Inoculation

45. The age period in which lack of proper nutrition results in the MOST harm is 45._____
    A. from birth to 6 years of age
    B. childhood (approximately 6-12 years)
    C. adolescence (approximately 12-18 years)
    D. early maturity (18-24 years)

KEY (CORRECT ANSWERS)

1. C	11. B	21. B	31. D	41. C
2. B	12. A	22. A	32. B	42. D
3. C	13. D	23. E	33. C	43. D
4. C	14. E	24. D	34. B	44. C
5. A	15. D	25. A	35. C	45. A
6. C	16. B	26. C	36. A	
7. B	17. A	27. C	37. A	
8. C	18. D	28. A	38. B	
9. C	19. D	29. C	39. A	
10. B	20. C	30. B	40. D	

26

EXAMINATION SECTION

TEST 1

DIRECTIONS: Each question or incomplete statement is followed by several suggested answers or completions. Select the one that BEST answers the question or completes the statement. *PRINT THE LETTER OF THE CORRECT ANSWER IN THE SPACE AT THE RIGHT.*

1. Dichloro-diphenyl-trichloroethane was used MOST effectively as a(n)   1.____
   A. disinfectant   B. termite preventative
   C. moth preventative   D. insecticide

2. Learning by constant repetition without being aware of the thought behind what is   2.____
   being learned is
   A. book learning   B. automation
   C. rationalization   D. rote learning

3. All of the following are common methods for treating drug addiction EXCEPT   3.____
   A. detoxification with guidance from healthcare professionals
   B. medication to manage cravings and withdrawal symptoms
   C. behavioral and psychological therapy
   D. institutionalization until the addiction is cured

4. The purpose of vaccines is to   4.____
   A. reduce the causative organism
   B. develop scar tissue
   C. stimulate growth of antibodies
   D. produce bacteriostasis

5. Of the following, the MOST dangerous narcotic is   5.____
   A. codeine   B. opium
   C. heroin   D. marijuana

6. If a teenage girl is careless about putting her clothes away,   6.____
   A. put the clothing away for her
   B. tolerate the situation
   C. inspire her to be neat
   D. lecture her

7. A two-year-old child that refuses to eat lunch should   7.____
   A. be forced to eat
   B. be appeased
   C. not be forced to eat, and the food should be removed without comment after
      a reasonable amount of time has passed
   D. be scolded

8. Thumbsucking should be eliminated by   8._____
   A. satisfying the physical and emotional needs
   B. mechanical restraints
   C. applying distatseful compounds
   D. punishment

9. During the first three years, the strongest influence on the personality of a child is   9._____
   A. his or her friends
   B. the economic status of the family
   C. the social status of the family
   D. his or her relationships within the family

10. For 12-year-old children, an allowance   10._____
    A. may be used as a training device
    B. should be provided
    C. encourages a distorted sense of values
    D. provides a means of disciplinary control

11. When a 10-year-old boy temporarily becomes irritable and boisterous, parents should   11._____
    A. divert his attention   B. punish him
    C. cater to his whims   D. ascertain the reason

12. Parents should provide opportunities to habituate control of small muscles of the   12._____
    arms when the child
    A. eats solid food   B. makes an effort to feed himself
    C. eats in restaurant   D. attends school

13. Concerning a six-year-old child, parents who insist on absolute perfection may   13._____
    A. hamper future accomplishments
    B. encourage good habits
    C. increase mutual love
    D. destroy imitative performance

14. Lefthandedness   14._____
    A. is an individual trait   B. should be corrected
    C. indicates a shortcoming   D. is a conditioned reflex

15. To reduce fears in children, parents should   15._____
    A. give affection   B. lecture them
    C. shield them   D. provide safeguards

16. When a new baby is expected, to encourage a sense of belonging, older children   16._____
    should be allowed
    A. to anticipate another playmate
    B. no knowledge of the new baby
    C. to know, but not talk, about the new baby
    D. to share in the preparations

17. First-aid care of a third-degree burn requires   17.____
    - A. oil and chalk mixture   B. sterile dressing
    - C. antiseptic solution   D. healing ointment

18. Concerning teeth,   18.____
    - A. dental caries appear most frequently between ages 12 and 20
    - B. dental tartar should not be removed
    - C. orthodontia is unimportant
    - D. fluorides prevent all decay

19. Heat destroys bacteria by   19.____
    - A. enucleation
    - B. hemolysis
    - C. coagulating protein
    - D. making the cell wall permeable

20. The value of antihistaminic compounds lies PRIMARILY in their ability to   20.____
    - A. increase intervals between infections
    - B. relieve allergic manifestations
    - C. immunize
    - D. prevent the spread of infection

21. A test program that gives positive proof of drug addiction is through the use of   21.____
    - A. hystidine   B. nalline   C. chlorine   D. choline

22. Drug withdrawal symptoms in addicts include vomiting and changes in   22.____
    - A. muscular control   B. nerves
    - C. color of the skin   D. pupils of the eyes

23. Overuse of NSAIDs like ibuprofen often leads to   23.____
    - A. allergic reaction
    - B. memory loss or dizziness
    - C. sharp decrease in blood pressure
    - D. gastrointestinal issues

24. Plantar fasciitis is a condition most likely to be diagnosed by a(n)   24.____
    - A. dermatologist   B. hand specialist
    - C. oncologist   D. podiatrist

25. Body Mass Index (BMI) is a numeric value used to classify patients as   25.____
    overweight or obese through the measurement of _____ and _____.
    - A. height; weight   B. HDL; LDL
    - C. pulse rate; breathing rate   D. weight; cholesterol

26. The home can BEST benefit the mental health of its members through   26.____
    - A. development of attitudes which result in appropriate emotional expression
    - B. an elementary knowledge of psychiatry
    - C. a check on the psychosomatics of the older members
    - D. regular physical check-ups

27. When a child expresses fear of darkness on retiring, the BEST procedure is to   27.____
    A. make light of his fears
    B. compel him to accept the darkness
    C. provide a dim light
    D. shame him for his fears

28. Active immunity is acquired through   28.____
    A. production of antibodies
    B. imperviousness of skin tissue
    C. enzyme activity
    D. washing action of mucous membranes

29. The main criticism of body mass index as a measure of overall health is that it   29.____
    A. can cause mental health issues by classifying someone as obese
    B. fails to accurately account for muscle mass and body fat
    C. is too complex to provide an accurate assessment
    D. is too difficult to measure

30. A highly dangerous and addictive synthetic narcotic is   30.____
    A. amidol   B. amidone   C. cobalamine   D. pyridoxine

———————

KEY (CORRECT ANSWERS)

1.	D	11.	D	21.	B
2.	D	12.	B	22.	D
3.	D	13.	A	23.	D
4.	C	14.	A	24.	D
5.	C	15.	A	25.	A
6.	C	16.	D	26.	A
7.	C	17.	B	27.	C
8.	A	18.	A	28.	A
9.	D	19.	C	29.	B
10.	A	20.	B	30.	B

———————

TEST 2

DIRECTIONS: Each question or incomplete statement is followed by several suggested answers or completions. Select the one that BEST answers the question or completes the statement. *PRINT THE LETTER OF THE CORRECT ANSWER IN THE SPACE AT THE RIGHT.*

1. The Salk vaccine is administered to prevent
   A. measles
   B. diphtheria
   C. poliomyelitis
   D. whooping cough

   1._____

2. Cancer of the blood is
   A. carcinoma
   B. sarcoma
   C. leukemia
   D. epithelioma

   2._____

3. The accepted treatment in severe and extensive radiation burns is to FIRST
   A. apply tannic acid generously
   B. apply wet sodium bicarbonate dressing
   C. bandage the burned area firmly
   D. put the patient to bed

   3._____

4. A bed cradle is a device for supporting the
   A. back
   B. knees
   C. bed covering
   D. food tray

   4._____

5. Pediculosis Capitus refers to
   A. baldness
   B. athlete's foot
   C. lice
   D. tics

   5._____

6. The MAIN purpose of a good nursing chart is to
   A. aid the nurse's memory
   B. help the doctor in diagnosis and treatment
   C. prevent lawsuits
   D. protect the hospital

   6._____

7. When an ice bag is applied, it should be
   A. kept filled with ice
   B. strapped in place
   C. removed every 15 or 20 minutes
   D. removed every hour

   7._____

8. Hepatitis is a disease of the
   A. renals
   B. spleen
   C. liver
   D. pancreas

   8._____

9. Bones are joined to one another with
   A. sinews
   B. tendons
   C. ligaments
   D. membranes

   9._____

10. Average adult pulse rate for a man is   10.____
    A. 64   B. 72   C. 80   D. 96

11. In MOST cases, to get a doctor in an emergency, call the   11.____
    A. nearest doctor   B. nearest hospital
    C. Red Cross   D. police emergency 911

12. Intravenous injections may be legally administered by the   12.____
    A. registered nurse   B. practical nurse
    C. nursing aide   D. home nurse

13. Persons who are likely to come in contact with communicable diseases are   13.____
immunized by
    A. heredity   B. environment
    C. asepsis   D. biotics

14. The temperature of water for a hot water bottle should NOT exceed   14.____
    A. 100°F   B. 150°F   C. 125°F   D. 175°F

15. The currently accepted treatment for arthritis is   15.____
    A. x-ray   B. cortisone
    C. aureomycin   D. gold injections

16. The MOST reliable temperature is that found in the   16.____
    A. rectum   B. axilla
    C. mouth   D. none of the above

17. An antiseptic solution recommended in first aid for slight skin scratches (abrasions) is   17.____
    A. concentrated boric acid
    B. tincture of merthiolate 1:1000
    C. iodine 2%
    D. tincture of green soap

18. The MOST frequent cause of death in the United States today is   18.____
    A. cancer   B. tuberculosis
    C. Alzheimer's disease   D. heart disease

19. Average adult temperature by rectum is ____°F.   19.____
    A. 99.6   B. 97.6   C. 98.6   D. 100.6

20. Metaplasia refers to disturbances of the   20.____
    A. mucous membranes   B. epithelial tissues
    C. cartilage   D. basal metabolism

21. A subjective symptom is one that the patient   21.____
    A. feels   B. hears
    C. sees   D. smells

22. A bed cradle
    A. keeps the patient's weight off the bed
    B. keeps the knees up
    C. elevates the feet
    D. keeps the weight of the covers off the patient

22.____

23. Statistics indicate that MOST youths start the drug habit with
    A. marijuana   B. heroin   C. cocaine   D. morphine

23.____

24. A stroke may be caused by
    A. cerebral hemorrhage   B. caecal dilation
    C. aortal thrombosis   D. pleural edema

24.____

25. The control of automatic breathing is located in the
    A. cerebrum   B. cerebellum
    C. spinal cord   D. medulla oblongata

25.____

26. The water for a baby's bath should be closest to ____°F.
    A. 80   B. 90   C. 100   D. 110

26.____

27. The Schick test indicates immunity to
    A. diphtheria   B. smallpox   C. tetanus   D. tuberculosis

27.____

28. Difficulty in speaking is known as
    A. asphyxia   B. aphasia   C. amnesia   D. anorexia

28.____

29. A water blister should be
    A. opened and drained
    B. left unbroken
    C. painted with iodine and bandaged
    D. soaked in hot Epsom salt solution

29.____

30. The FIRST to be affected by the anesthetizing action of alcohol is the exercise of
    A. judgment   B. memory
    C. muscular coordination   D. control of speech

30.____

31. To the nervous system, alcohol acts as a
    A. depressant   B. stimulant   C. gratifier   D. agitator

31.____

32. Acute alcoholism may properly be labeled a psychosis because it involves
    A. intellectual limitations
    B. a loss of contact with reality
    C. emotional inadequacies
    D. bodily disease

32.____

33. Blood alcohol content is a measure of 33.____
    A. the amount of alcohol consumed in a 24-hour span
    B. the amount of alcohol in the blood
    C. the amount of alcohol it takes to intoxicate an average adult
    D. the effect of alcohol on blood thinning

34. Characteristic symptoms of chronic alcoholism include 34.____
    A. exiccosis
    B. damage to brain tissue
    C. increase in weight
    D. periods of depression

35. Alcohol is MOST often used excessively in order to 35.____
    A. induce sleep
    B. stimulate brain action
    C. overcome social inadequacy
    D. furnish temporary release from tensions

KEY (CORRECT ANSWERS)

1.	C	11.	D	21.	A	31.	A
2.	C	12.	A	22.	D	32.	B
3.	C	13.	D	23.	A	33.	B
4.	C	14.	C	24.	A	34.	D
5.	C	15.	B	25.	D	35.	D
6.	B	16.	A	26.	C		
7.	C	17.	C	27.	A		
8.	C	18.	D	28.	B		
9.	C	19.	C	29.	B		
10.	B	20.	C	30.	A		

EXAMINATION SECTION
TEST 1

DIRECTIONS: Each question or incomplete statement is followed by several suggested answers or completions. Select the one that BEST answers the question or completes the statement. *PRINT THE LETTER OF THE CORRECT ANSWER IN THE SPACE AT THE RIGHT.*

Questions 1-4.

DIRECTIONS: Questions 1 through 4 are to be answered on the basis of the following information.

In a day care center of 30 children (20 females and 10 males), 7 boys develop hepatitis A over a 3-week period. During the next 8 weeks, an additional 2 boys and 5 girls develop the infection.

1. The attack rate of hepatitis A in this day care center is _____%.   1._____
    A. 20   B. 30   C. 40   D. 46.6   E. 54.5

2. The secondary attack rate of hepatitis A in this day care center is MOST NEARLY   2._____
    _____%.
    A. 20   B. 15   C. 23   D. 27   E. 10

3. The attack rate of hepatitis A for boys in this school is MOST NEARLY _____%.   3._____
    A. 16   B. 40   C. 50   D. 60   E. 64

4. The attack rate of hepatitis A for girls is MOST NEARLY _____%.   4._____
    A. 21   B. 24   C. 25   D. 27   E. 30

5. The epidemic curve suggests a common source outbreak with   5._____

    A. continuing common source outbreak
    B. fecal-oral transmission
    C. secondary airborne transmission
    D. secondary person-to-person transmission
    E. none of the above

6. The _____ rate is determined by the number of deaths caused by a specific disease   6._____
    divided by the number of cases of the disease.

    A. mortality   B. case fatality
    C. attack   D. cause specific death
    E. none of the above

7. Rate is the expression of the probability of occurrence of a particular event in a defined   7._____
    population during a specified period of time.
    The rate calculated for various segments of the population is known as the _____
    rate.

    A. specific   B. crude
    C. adjusted   D. variable
    E. none of the above

8. The sources of disease surveillance data include all of the following EXCEPT   8.____

   A. individual case reports
   B. emergency room visit records
   C. hospital discharge summaries
   D. death certificates
   E. none of the above

9. All of the following are true about tularemia EXCEPT that it is   9.____

   A. a zoonotic disease
   B. more common during the summer months in the western states
   C. more common in winter months in the eastern states
   D. primarily transmitted by the bite of a spider
   E. none of the above

10. Which of the following is NOT among the basic steps in an investigation of an epidemic?   10.____

   A. Verification of diagnosis
   B. Establishing the existence of an epidemic
   C. Characterization of the distribution of cases
   D. Formulating a conclusion
   E. All of the above

11. The LAST step in conducting an epidemic investigation is to   11.____

   A. develop an hypothesis
   B. test the hypothesis
   C. formulate a conclusion
   D. institute control measures
   E. establish the diagnosis of an epidemic

12. The patients who are infected with an agent but never develop clinical symptoms of the disease are known as _____ carriers.   12.____

   A. incubatory   B. subclinical   C. chronic
   D. convalescent   E. clinical

13. All of the following are uses of epidemiology EXCEPT to   13.____

   A. identify factors that cause disease
   B. explain how and why diseases and epidemics occur
   C. establish a clinical diagnosis of disease
   D. determine a patient's prognosis
   E. evaluate the effectiveness of health programs

14. The biological traits that determine the occurrence of a disease include all of the following EXCEPT   14.____

   A. genetic characteristics   B. diet
   C. race   D. ethnic origin
   E. sex

15. The general factors of resistance in a human host include all of the following EXCEPT   15.____

    A. the immune system   B. intact skin
    C. diarrhea   D. normal bacterial flora
    E. gastric juices

16. All of the following are examples of direct contact transmission EXCEPT   16.____

    A. syphilis   B. herpes
    C. hepatitis B   D. sporotrichosis
    E. none of the above

17. The basic aims and specific goals of medical studies and clinical research do NOT include   17.____

    A. assessing health status or clinical characteristics
    B. eliminating all carriers of diseases
    C. determining and assessing treatment outcomes
    D. identifying and assessing risk factors
    E. all of the above

18. Incidence and prevalence studies usually concern all of the following EXCEPT   18.____

    A. the occurrence of disease
    B. a comparison of outcomes between different treatments
    C. adverse side effects of drugs
    D. the death rate for a certain disease
    E. none of the above

19. A case series report can address almost any clinical issue but it is MOST commonly used to describe   19.____

    A. clinical characteristics of a disease
    B. screening test results
    C. treatment outcomes
    D. an unexpected result or event
    E. none of the above

20. A comparison of chemotherapy to chemotherapy plus radiation for laryngeal carcinoma would be an appropriate topic for a(n)   20.____

    A. cohort study
    B. case control study
    C. clinical trial
    D. case series report
    E. incidence and prevalence study

21. The sum of all values in a series divided by the actual number of values in the series is known as the   21.____

    A. mode   B. median
    C. geometric mean   D. arithmetic mean
    E. none of the above

22. The MOST commonly occurring value in a series of values is the

    22.____

    A. mode
    B. median
    C. geometric mean
    D. arithmetic mean
    E. none of the above

23. The ratio of the standard deviation of a series to the arithmetic mean of the series is known as the

    23.____

    A. range
    B. variance
    C. coefficient of variation
    D. standard deviation
    E. epidemic curve

24. The sum of squared deviations from the mean divided by the number of values in the series minus 1 is called the

    24.____

    A. range
    B. variance
    C. standard deviation
    D. coefficient of variation
    E. frequency polygon

25. The _____ is a tool for comparing categories of mutually exclusive discrete data.

    25.____

    A. pie chart
    B. Venn diagram
    C. bar diagram
    D. histogram
    E. frequency polygon

KEY (CORRECT ANSWERS)

1.	D	11	D
2.	C	12.	B
3.	E	13.	D
4.	C	14.	B
5.	D	15.	A
6.	B	16.	E
7.	A	17.	B
8.	E	18.	B
9.	D	19.	A
10.	E	20.	C

21	D
22.	A
23.	C
24.	B
25.	C

TEST 2

DIRECTIONS: Each question or incomplete statement is followed by several suggested answers or completions. Select the one that BEST answers the question or completes the statement. *PRINT THE LETTER OF THE CORRECT ANSWER IN THE SPACE AT THE RIGHT.*

1. A _____ is a special form of the bar diagram used to represent categories of continuous and ordered data.   1._____

    A. pie chart
    B. histogram
    C. Venn diagram
    D. cumulative frequency graph
    E. frequency polygon

2. A medical student performs venipuncture on 1,000 randomly selected patients and is successful on the first attempt 700 times.
What is the probability that her next venipuncture will be successful on the first attempt?   2._____

    A. 7%   B. 14%   C. 50%   D. 70%   E. 80%

3. All of the following are true regarding the standard error of the mean of a sample EXCEPT that it   3._____

    A. is an estimate of the standard deviation of the population
    B. is based on a normal distribution
    C. increases as the sample size increases
    D. is used to determine confidence limits
    E. none of the above

4. All of the following are characteristics of a confidence interval EXCEPT that it   4._____

    A. is based on a critical ratio when the sample is large
    B. gives an indication of the likely magnitude of the true value
    C. gives an indication of the certainty of the point estimate
    D. becomes narrower as the sample size increases
    E. none of the above

5. Nonparametric tests can be used to compare two populations with which of the following conditions?   5._____

    A. Each population is unimodal
    B. Both populations have equal numbers
    C. Each population is independent
    D. Each population is distributed normally
    E. All of the above

6. All of the following vaccines are grown in embryonated chicken eggs EXCEPT   6._____

    A. yellow fever   B. measles   C. mumps
    D. rubella   E. influenza

7. Which of the following vaccines should NOT be given to individuals who live in house-   7.____
holds with an immuno-compromised host?

    A. Yellow fever   B. Hepatitis B   C. Oral polio
    D. Influenza   E. Diphtheriae

8. A solution of antibodies derived from the serum of animals immunized with a specific   8.____
antigen is a(n)

    A. immunoglobulin   B. antitoxin
    C. toxoid   D. vaccine
    E. none of the above

9. All of the following may be significant sequale of measles infection EXCEPT   9.____

    A. pneumonia
    B. encephalitis
    C. congenital birth defects
    D. mental retardation
    E. death

10. All of the following statements about vaccination during pregnancy are true EXCEPT: 10.____

    A. Live attenuated viral vaccines should not be given to pregnant women
    B. Pregnant women at substantial risk of exposure may receive a live viral vaccine
    C. There is evidence that inactivated vaccines also pose risks to the fetus
    D. There is no evidence that immunoglobulins pose any risk to the fetus
    E. None of the above

11. None of the following conditions are reasons for delaying or discontinuing routine immu-   11.____
nizations EXCEPT

    A. soreness, redness or swelling at the injection site in reaction to previous immuniza-
tion
    B. a temperature of more than 105F in reaction to previous DTP vaccine
    C. mild diarrheal illness in an otherwise well child
    D. current antimicrobial therapy
    E. breastfeeding

12. Children and infants with any of the following disorders should not receive pertussis vac-   12.____
cine EXCEPT those with

    A. uncontrolled epilepsy
    B. infantile spasms
    C. progressive encephalopathy
    D. developmental delay
    E. none of the above

13. Which of the following groups of patients should NOT receive pneumococcal polysaccha-   13.____
ride vaccine?

    A. Elderly, age 65 or older
    B. Immunocompromised
    C. Children age 2 years or older with anatomic or functional asplenia

D. Children age 2 years or older with nephrotic syndrome or CSF leaks
E. Children under 2 years of age

14. All of the following are significant complications of sexually transmitted diseases in women EXCEPT   14.____

A. pelvic inflammatory disease
B. infertility
C. teratogenicity
D. cancer
E. ectopic pregnancy

15. For primary prevention and maximal safety, a person should   15.____

A. engage in a mutually monogamous relationship
B. limit the number of sexual partners
C. inspect and question new partners
D. avoid sexual practices involving anal or fecal contact
E. all of the above

16. All of the following are complications caused by untreated syphilis infection EXCEPT   16.____

A. obesity   B. blindness
C. psychosis   D. cardiovascular disease
E. none of the above

17. All of the following statements are true regarding syphilis EXCEPT: 17.____

A. The organism cannot enter through intact skin
B. Everyone is susceptible
C. There is no natural or acquired immunity
D. No vaccine is available
E. Reinfection is rare

18. Which of the following sexually transmitted diseases rank as the number one reported communicable disease in the United States?   18.____

A. Syphilis   B. Gonorrhea   C. AIDS
D. Chlamydia   E. Hepatitis B

19. Which of the following is believed to be the MOST common sexually transmitted bacterial pathogen in the United States?   19.____

A. Treponema pallidum   B. Chlamydia trachomatis
C. Nisseriae gonorrhea   D. E. coli
E. Herpes zoster

20. All of the following are documented modes of transmission for human immunodeficiency virus EXCEPT _____ transmission.   20.____

A. sexual   B. percutaneous exposure
C. airborne   D. mother to child
E. none of the above

21. In order to prevent HIV infection, which of the following groups should NOT donate blood?   21.____

    A. Any man who has had sexual contact with another man since 1977
    B. Present or past IV drug abusers
    C. Individuals from Central Africa and Haiti
    D. Sexual partners of any of the above groups
    E. All of the above

22. Chlamydia trachomatis, the causative agent of chlamydia infection, has all of the following characteristics EXCEPT it   22.____

    A. grows only intracellularly
    B. contains both DNA and RNA
    C. is a protozoa
    D. divides by binary fission
    E. has cell walls similar to gram-negative bacteriae

23. All of the following are true regarding the resultant effects of chlamydia trachomatis EXCEPT: 23.____

    A. Approximately 50% cases of non-gonococcal urethritis in men
    B. 99% of cases of pelvic inflammatory disease
    C. Mucopurulent cervicitis
    D. Inclusion conjunctivitis in infants born to infected mothers
    E. Acute epididymitis in men

24. All of the following statements are true regarding hepatitis A infection EXCEPT: 24.____

    A. Approximately 70% of Americans are infected by the age of 20
    B. Incidence appears to be declining
    C. Infection is related to age and socioeconomic status
    D. The incubation period is 15-50 days with an average of 28-30 days
    E. Young children are more likely to have subclinical infections

25. The transmission of hepatitis A virus is facilitated by all of the following EXCEPT   25.____

    A. poor personal hygiene
    B. poor sanitation
    C. drinking out of the same cup
    D. eating uncooked or raw food
    E. eating food contaminated by human hands after cooking

KEY (CORRECT ANSWERS)

1.	B		11.	B
2.	D		12.	D
3.	C		13.	E
4.	E		14.	C
5.	E		15.	E
6.	D		16.	A
7.	C		17.	E
8.	B		18.	B
9.	C		19.	B
10.	C		20.	C

21.	E
22.	C
23.	B
24.	A
25.	C

———

EXAMINATION SECTION
TEST 1

DIRECTIONS: Each question or incomplete statement is followed by several suggested answers or completions. Select the one that BEST answers the question or completes the statement. *PRINT THE LETTER OF THE CORRECT ANSWER IN THE SPACE AT THE RIGHT.*

1. A PPD reaction of greater than or equal to 5 mm induration is considered positive in all of the following individuals EXCEPT   1.____

    A. persons with HIV infection
    B. IV drug abusers who are HIV antibody negative
    C. close recent contacts of an infectious tuberculosis case
    D. persons with a chest radiograph consistent with old, healed tuberculosis
    E. persons with HIV infection or with risk factors for HIV infection who have an unknown IV antibody status

2. All of the following are true about tuberculosis EXCEPT: 2.____

    A. The causative agent is M. tuberculosis var. hominis
    B. It is more likely to occur in older individuals (more than 45 years of age)
    C. It is more common in non-whites than in whites
    D. It is more common in men than in women
    E. About 90% of cases in the United States represent new infections

3. The groups that should benefit from preventive therapy for tuberculosis include all of the following EXCEPT   3.____

    A. individuals whose skin test has converted from negative to positive in the previous 2 years
    B. individuals with positive mantoux test and with HIV infection
    C. tuberculin-negative IV drug abusers
    D. tuberculin-positive individuals under 35 years of age
    E. individuals with immunosuppressive therapy who are tuberculin positive

4. INH prophylaxis should not be used in any of the following EXCEPT in   4.____

    A. the presence of clinical disease
    B. a pregnant woman who has recently converted to tuberculin positive
    C. patients with unstable hepatic function
    D. individuals who were previously adequately treated
    E. individuals with a previous adverse reaction to INH

5. What is the MOST common cause of bacterial meningitis in children under age 5?   5.____

    A. Streptococcus pneumoniae
    B. H. influenza
    C. N. meningitidis
    D. E. coli
    E. Staphylococcus aureus

6. All of the following are true about H. influenza infection EXCEPT: 6.____

    A. Peak incidence is from age 3 months to 2 years
    B. The mortality rate is about 5%
    C. Secondary spread to day care contacts under 4 years of age is rare
    D. About two-thirds of the cases occur in children under 15 months of age
    E. None of the above

7. All of the following statements are true about hemophilus influenza type B infection EXCEPT: 7.____

    A. Rifampin is the drug of choice for chemoprophylaxis
    B. Rifampin may be given to pregnant women
    C. The disease is more common in native and black Americans
    D. Humans are the reservoir of infections
    E. None of the above

8. All of the following statements are true about meningococcal meningitis EXCEPT: 8.____

    A. It is the second most common cause of bacterial meningitis in the United States
    B. The peak incidence is around age 6-12 months
    C. Most cases occur in late winter and early spring
    D. The portal of entry is not the nasopharynx
    E. It is more likely to occur in newly aggregated young adults who are living in institutions and barracks

9. Antimicrobial chemoprophylaxis is the chief preventive measure in sporadic cases of meningococcal meningitis and should be offered to   9.____

    A. household contacts
    B. day care center contacts
    C. medical personnel who resuscitated, intubated or suctioned the patient before antibiotics were instituted
    D. all patients who were treated for meningococcal disease before discharge from the hospital
    E. all of the above

10. What is the MOST common cause of bacterial meningitis in children under 5 years of age?   10.____

    A. Streptococcus pneumoniae
    B. Nisseriae meningitidis
    C. Listeria monocytogenes
    D. Group B streptococcus
    E. Hemophilus influenza type B

11. All of the following are true about coronary heart disease EXCEPT: 11.____

    A. It is the leading cause of death in the United States
    B. About 4.6 million Americans have coronary heart disease
    C. It is most common in white men
    D. Women have a greater risk of myocardial infarction and sudden death
    E. Women have a greater risk of angina pectoris

12. According to the National Cholesterol Education Panel, which of the following is NOT a major risk factor for coronary artery disease?   12.____

    A. Women 55 years and older
    B. Hypertension
    C. Individuals with diabetes mellitus
    D. High density lipoprotein (HDL) less than 35 mg/dl
    E. Obesity

13. The number one cause of cancer death in the United States is _____ cancer.   13.____

    A. lung   B. breast   C. colorectal
    D. cervical   E. prostatic

14. The MOST common cancer in American men is _____ cancer.   14.____

    A. lung   B. breast   C. prostate
    D. colon   E. esophageal

15. All of the following are risk factors for women to develop breast cancer EXCEPT   15.____

    A. exposure to ionizing radiation
    B. becoming pregnant for the first time after age 30
    C. mother and sisters having breast cancer
    D. high socioeconomic status
    E. late menarchae

16. Cervical cancer is one of the leading causes of death among women. Of the following, which is NOT a risk factor for developing cervical cancer?   16.____

    A. Multiple sexual partners
    B. First coitus before age 20
    C. Low socioeconomic status
    D. Oral contraceptive use
    E. Partners of uncircumcised men

17. Population subgroups at INCREASED risk of developing anemia include   17.____

    A. women   B. elderly men
    C. children   D. blacks
    E. all of the above

18. Uncontrolled hypertensive disease increases the risk of developing all of the following disorders EXCEPT   18.____

    A. coronary heart disease   B. diabetes mellitus
    C. renal disease   D. cerebrovascular disease
    E. none of the above

19. All of the following statements are true regarding chronic obstructive pulmonary disease (COPD) EXCEPT: 19.____

    A. Men are at higher risk than women
    B. An estimated 16 million Americans have chronic bronchitis, asthma or emphysema
    C. The risk is related to the duration of smoking only

D. The risk is related to the number of cigarettes smoked daily and to the duration of smoking
E. Offspring of affected individuals are at higher risk

20. Which of the following statements is TRUE regarding diabetes in the United States?   20._____

    A. It accounts for 5% of all deaths.
    B. Its prevalence is estimated at 15%.
    C. 80% of all diabetics have the non-insulin dependent type.
    D. It is the leading cause of blindness.
    E. Men are at greater risk than women.

21. People with increased risk for suicide include all of the following EXCEPT   21._____

    A. drug users   B. married individuals
    C. teenagers   D. chronically depressed
    E. homosexuals

22. Conditions associated with an increased risk for suicide include all of the following EXCEPT   22._____

    A. unemployed
    B. seriously physically ill or handicapped
    C. chronically mentally ill
    D. substance abusers
    E. none of the above

23. The leading cause of death among black men aged 15-24 years is   23._____

    A. automobile accidents   B. homicide
    C. cancer   D. drug abuse
    E. AIDS

24. All of the following are true regarding pernicious anemia EXCEPT: 24._____

    A. It primarily affects individuals over the age of 30
    B. The incidence increases with age
    C. It is more common in Asians and blacks
    D. It is caused by a vitamin B_{12} deficiency
    E. None of the above

25. Which of the following groups of individuals have a high risk of injuries?   25._____

    A. Factory workers
    B. Alcoholics
    C. Individuals with osteoporosis
    D. Homeless
    E. All of the above

KEY (CORRECT ANSWERS)

1.	B	11.	D
2.	E	12.	D
3.	C	13.	A
4.	B	14.	C
5.	B	15.	E
6.	C	16.	C
7.	B	17.	E
8.	D	18.	B
9.	E	19.	C
10.	E	20.	D

21.	B
22.	E
23.	B
24.	C
25.	E

TEST 2

DIRECTIONS: Each question or incomplete statement is followed by several suggested answers or completions. Select the one that BEST answers the question or completes the statement. *PRINT THE LETTER OF THE CORRECT ANSWER IN THE SPACE AT THE RIGHT.*

1. Which of the following factors does NOT increase a woman's risk of an ectopic pregnancy?   1.____

   A. Progestin exposure
   B. Pelvic inflammatory disease
   C. Smoking
   D. Use of alcohol
   E. Infertility

2. Breastfeeding usually enhances all of the following EXCEPT   2.____

   A. bonding between mother and infant
   B. infant nutrition
   C. immune defenses
   D. antibody response against HIV virus
   E. return of uterus to prepregnant size

3. Which of the following is NOT a leading cause of maternal mortality in the United States?   3.____

   A. Hypertensive disease of pregnancy
   B. Cardiovascular accidents
   C. Miscarriage
   D. Anesthesia complications
   E. All of the above

4. A well-woman prenatal visit should include all of the following EXCEPT a(n)   4.____

   A. weight check
   B. blood pressure check
   C. electronic fetal monitoring
   D. pap smear
   E. urine analysis

5. All of the following substances or conditions are harmful to the fetus during gestation EXCEPT   5.____

   A. tetracycline   B. alcohol   C. herpes
   D. rubella   E. thalidomide

6. The use of an intrauterine device (IUD) has been associated with increased risk of   6.____

   A. ectopic pregnancy
   B. pelvic inflammatory disease
   C. infertility
   D. infections
   E. all of the above

7. The number of deaths among infants less than 28 days old per 1,000 live births is called   7._____
the _____ mortality rate.

    A. neonatal   B. post-neonatal
    C. fetal   D. perinatal
    E. none of the above

8. All of the following are causes of postneonatal mortality EXCEPT   8._____

    A. lower respiratory tract infections
    B. intrauterine growth retardation
    C. congenital anomalies
    D. sudden infant death syndrome
    E. injuries, e.g., motor vehicle accidents

9. All of the following are important factors in the identification of high risk parents and in the   9._____
management and prevention of infant health problems EXCEPT

    A. intrauterine infections
    B. pre-existing maternal illnesses
    C. paternal age
    D. maternal history of reproductive problems
    E. family history of hereditary disease

10. Screening for which of the following conditions has been proven to be cost effective?   10._____

    A. Phenylketonuria   B. Congenital hypothyroidism
    C. Lead poisoning   D. Tuberculosis
    E. All of the above

11. Children _____ are more likely to receive inadequate well-child care.   11._____

    A. with chronic health problems
    B. on medicaid
    C. of mothers who started receiving prenatal care late in the second or third trimester
    D. of parents whose jobs do not provide health insurance
    E. all of the above

12. Injuries are classified by the intent or purposefulness of occurrence.   12._____
All of the following are classified as intentional injuries EXCEPT

    A. child abuse   B. motor vehicle mishaps
    C. sexual assault   D. domestic violence
    E. abuse of the elderly

13. Schizophrenia is a disorder, or group of disorders, with a variety of symptoms that   13._____
include

    A. delusions   B. hallucinations
    C. agitation   D. apathy
    E. all of the above

14. All of the following are true about the incidence and prevalence of bipolar disorder   14._____
EXCEPT:

51

A. Approximately 4-5% of the population is at risk
B. More women are admitted to the hospital with the diagnosis of bipolar disorder than men
C. The manic form occurs primarily in younger individuals
D. Bipolar patients are more likely to be unmarried
E. The depressive form occurs primarily in older individuals

15. In schizophrenia, there is an increased risk for all of the following EXCEPT   15.____

    A. malabsorption syndrome
    B. arteriosclerotic heart disease
    C. hypothyroidism
    D. cancer
    E. none of the above

16. A 6-month-old Jewish infant has a history of seizures, progressive blindness, deafness,   16.____
and paralysis with an exaggerated startle response to sound.
The MOST likely diagnosis is

    A. phenylketonuria   B. Gaucher's disease
    C. Tay Sachs disease   D. homocystinuria
    E. maple syrup disease

17. The MOST common inborn error of amino acid metabolism results in   17.____

    A. phenylketonuria   B. maple syrup disease
    C. homocystinuria   D. albinism
    E. Gaucher's disease

18. The MOST common lysosomal storage disease is   18.____

    A. Niemann-Pick disease   B. Gaucher's disease
    C. Tay Sachs disease   D. homocystinuria
    E. none of the above

19. All of the following are true about spina bifida EXCEPT: 19.____

    A. The most common type is spina bifida occulta
    B. The least severe form is myelocoele
    C. Encephalocoele is the rarest type
    D. The most common site affected is lower back
    E. The familial risk of recurrence is approximately 5%

Questions 20-25.

DIRECTIONS: For each metal listed in Questions 20 through 25, select the condition in the column below that is MOST likely to result from chronic exposure to it.

20. Lead	A. Osteomalacia-like disease		20.___
21. Arsenic	B. Granulomas of skin and lungs		21.___
22. Cadmium	C. Abnormal sperms		22.___
23. Mercury	D. Nasal septal ulceration		23.___
24. Beryllium	E. Visual field abnormalities		24.___
25. Zinc	F. Metal fume fever		25.___

KEY (CORRECT ANSWERS)

1.	D		11.	E
2.	D		12.	B
3.	C		13.	E
4.	C		14.	D
5.	C		15.	D
6.	E		16.	C
7.	A		17.	A
8.	B		18.	C
9.	C		19.	B
10.	E		20.	C

21.	D
22.	A
23.	E
24.	B
25.	F

EXAMINATION SECTION
TEST 1

DIRECTIONS: Each question or incomplete statement is followed by several suggested answers or completions. Select the one the BEST answers the question or completes the statement. *PRINT THE LETTER OF THE CORRECT ANSWER IN THE SPACE AT THE RIGHT.*

1. A health educator helps collect data for an epidemiological study that will examine the relationship, during the months of December and January, between the incidence of influenza in a community and the behaviors of the community members. The type of study to be conducted will be

    A. longitudinal
    B. ex post facto
    C. cross-sectional
    D. pre-test/post-test

1.____

2. In a worksite wellness program, which of the following is LEAST likely to help employees change their health risks?

    A. The use of "engagement" strategies that are individually designed
    B. A solid and focused array of health improvement classes and seminars
    C. Repeated follow-up contacts after programs or classes have ended
    D. Persistent, personalized outreach to at-risk employees

2.____

3. The final phase of the PRECEDE model of planning health education is the _____ diagnosis.

    A. behavioral
    B. administrative
    C. educational
    D. social

3.____

4. Typically, a health promotion effort in a community should begin with a(n)

    A. enhancement of community awareness about the program
    B. behavioral change strategy
    C. screening and appraisal of health risks
    D. socioemotional intervention

4.____

5. Role-playing exercises are sometimes a useful means of instruction in health education. Generally, a disadvantage associated with this activity is that it

    A. focuses on a narrow band of skills
    B. tends to truncate discussions
    C. makes learning more abstract
    D. requires a well-trained facilitator

5.____

6. In researching a community profile, which of the following items of information would probably be LEAST useful to a health educator?

    A. Average educational level of residents
    B. Age distribution

6.____

C. Political affiliations
D. Average household income

7. A health educator decides that in conducting a course for young teenagers on the dan-   7._____
gers of unprotected sex, he will adopt a paternalistic communication style. A potential
disadvantage associated with this decision is that

    A. attention is often diverted from real problems
    B. clients may become reluctant to take independent action
    C. clients may become likely to rebel or reject the views of the health educator
    D. the health educator may be perceived as neither supportive nor caring

8. To help conduct effective meetings, health educators and other program members   8._____
should

    A. begin only when all members of the group are present
    B. record minutes of each meeting and distribute them before the next
    C. take collective responsibility for tasks and deadlines
    D. let people raise issues that are important to them, even if they are not on the
       agenda

9. Though the cultural groups that make up the broad category known as "Asian American"   9._____
are varied in their beliefs and customs, it should generally be expected that first-genera-
tion immigrants from Asia will share a set of traditional values and behavior. Which of the
following would be LEAST likely to be included in these values and behaviors?

    A. Assertive help-seeking in time of need
    B. Blame of self for failure
    C. Control of strong feelings
    D. Respect for authority

10. As a general rule, sentences that appear in a health education brochure should each   10._____
contain about _____ or fewer words.

    A. 8
    B. 12
    C. 17
    D. 25

11. A health educator is participating in the writing of a grant proposal for a hygiene aware-   11._____
ness program for migrant workers. Typically, the body of a proposal should FIRST contain

    A. specific goals and objectives of the program
    B. a description of the target population
    C. an itemized budget for the program, including all expenses and a justification for
       each
    D. a one-page summary of the entire proposal

12. When defining and organizing a message for an adult audience with limited reading   12._____
skills, a health educator should NOT

    A. put the most important information in the middle of the presentation
    B. present one idea on a single page, or two facing pages

C. frequently summarize or repeat concepts

D. start with the completed idea one wants understood, then provide a breakdown or explanation

13. Which of the following theories would be MOST helpful in designing a program for treating alcohol abuse?   13.____

    A. Consensus

    B. Innovation-diffusion

    C. Conflict

    D. Self-regulation

14. As a mass media channel for the communication of a health-related message or public service announcement, magazines   14.____

    A. are more approachable and involve easier placement of PSAs than audiovisual media

    B. do not enable agencies to more specifically target segments of the public

    C. can explain more complex health issues and behaviors

    D. generally involve passive consumption

15. Which of the following is a risk factor associated with stroke?   15.____

    A. Alcohol abuse

    B. Obesity

    C. Home hazards

    D. Infectious agents

16. Before deciding upon a means of instruction, a health educator should know that people generally retain only about 10 percent of content that they   16.____

    A. say

    B. read

    C. do

    D. hear

17. For participants in a breast and cervical cancer control program, a health educator adapted a low-literacy flier developed by another organization. The flier was pre-tested among community members, and found to be written at the appropriate level. Staff at the agency observed that women in the program, after receiving the fliers, folded them to fit them in their purses, and many women left the fliers behind in the clinic. The most appropriate next step would be to   17.____

    A. conduct a focus group to discover what kind of format women would prefer for written information

    B. modify the format but keep the original text, to produce a flier that will fit into a woman's purse

    C. discontinue production of the fliers, and instead rely on visual presentation of the material on-site

    D. monitor the women as they leave the clinic and encourage them to take the flier with them

18. As part of a community assessment, a health educator wants to conduct a focus group   18.____
interview. The ideal number of members to participate in this sort of group is usually
about

    A. 3 to 5
    B. 4 to 8
    C. 10 to 12
    D. 15 to 20

19. In the client-centered model of health education, interventions are best described as   19.____

    A. promotion of medical interventions to prevent or alleviate ill health
    B. instruction about the causes and effects of health-demoting factors
    C. changing clients' attitudes and behaviors to promote the adoption of a healthier lifestyle
    D. collaborations with clients to identify and act on health-related concerns

20. Each of the following is a guideline that should be used in acquiring information from clients who are of different cultural or language backgrounds, EXCEPT   20.____

    A. asking questions in the exact same way repeatedly, to ensure understanding
    B. adjusting the style of the interaction to reflect differences in age between oneself and the client
    C. establishing rapport and showing genuine warm concern for the client, to build trust
    D. using open-ended questions to increase the amount of information obtained

21. The local newspaper has just run a story about a homeless encampment near the downtown area of a small city. An educator with the local health agency wants to write a letter to the editor of the paper, in order to draw attention to the services it offers to homeless people in the community. Guidelines for writing letters to be printed on the editorial page include   21.____
    I. the most important point should be made at the end of the letter
    II. letters should be saved for the most important issues
    III. letters should be signed by an officer of the organization
    IV. they should be no longer than 50-100 words

    A. I and II
    B. II and III
    C. III and IV
    D. I, II, III and IV

22. The lead agency in a coalition for health education and promotion should usually expect extensive staff demands in each of the following areas, EXCEPT   22.____

    A. clerical
    B. service delivery
    C. fund-raising
    D. research and fact gathering

23. A health agency conducts a readability test on one of its brochures. This is a(n) _____ 23.____
evaluation of a health education procedure.

    A. impact
    B. process
    C. outcome
    D. formative

24. Most nationwide initiatives focusing on public health, such as Healthy People 2000, place 24.____
the highest priority on

    A. physical activity and fitness
    B. family planning
    C. occupational safety and health
    D. violent and abusive behavior

25. A health educator designs a number of goals for his exercise education program, begin- 25.____
ning at the individual consciousness level and moving to social change. The educator will
have accomplished a decision-making change goal if, after completing the program, a client can say that she

    A. feels unfit because she gets out of breath easily
    B. will take fitness classes
    C. states the belief that she would feel better if she exercised more
    D. now goes to the gym regularly and is generally more physically active

_____

KEY (CORRECT ANSWERS)

1.	C		11.	D
2.	B		12.	A
3.	B		13.	D
4.	C		14.	C
5.	D		15.	A
6.	C		16.	B
7.	B		17.	B
8.	B		18.	C
9.	A		19.	D
10.	C		20.	A

21.	B
22.	B
23.	D
24.	A
25.	B

_____

TEST 2

DIRECTIONS: Each question or incomplete statement is followed by several suggested answers or completions. Select the one the BEST answers the question or completes the statement. *PRINT THE LETTER OF THE CORRECT ANSWER IN THE SPACE AT THE RIGHT.*

1. Which of the following is an example of secondary health education?   1.____

    A.   Demonstrating the proper installation of a child car seat
    B.   Explaining to a group of teens how to avoid contracting sexually transmitted diseases such as AIDS
    C.   Showing clients how to give first aid after an accident
    D.   Teaching a client with food allergies how to adjust eating habits to ensure minimum complications

2. A health educator wants to print a brochure on safe sex to be distributed among local   2.____
teenagers. The educator should know that the greatest expense involved in printing materials is

    A.   making the printing plates
    B.   paper
    C.   distribution costs
    D.   original artwork or graphics

3. In the beginning phase of a health education program, a good needs assessment pro-   3.____
cess can help the program designers to do each of the following, EXCEPT to

    A.   identify which programs to implement first
    B.   identify the types of programs needed
    C.   establish a set of baseline data to demonstrate later improvements
    D.   establish incentives for behavioral change

4. The most common mistake health educators make in designing a worksite wellness pro-   4.____
gram is to

    A.   depend solely on a schedule of classes for health improvement intervention
    B.   focus only on at-risk employees
    C.   use the "menu approach" to offering a variety of programs
    D.   spend too much time tracking down employees to persuade them to take part in programs or classes

5. A health educator working in a Hispanic/Latino community should remember that the   5.____
diverse Hispanic cultures in America tend to share some common values and behaviors. Which of the following is NOT one of these?

    A.   Family as the primary source of emotional and psychological support.
    B.   Matriarchal family structures.
    C.   Consultation with several family members before seeking health care.
    D.   Modesty and personal privacy.

6. Which of the following interventions does NOT conform to the medical model of health education?   6._____

    A. Persuading parents to bring their children in for vaccinations
    B. Teaching a course on how to care for teeth and gums
    C. Participating in a self-help group to discuss the issue of menopause
    D. Screening middle-aged men for high blood pressure

7. Of the following, which element should typically appear FIRST in the body of a proposal for the funding of a public health education program?   7._____

    A. The specific methods that will be used to meet program objectives-approach, action plan, timeline
    B. Process and outcome measures to be used in evaluating project success
    C. Brief background of the problem in the community, with supporting data
    D. The management plan for the project, including key staff members and their roles

8. At the local high school, a health educator is conducting a workshop on the dangers of certain commonly abused drugs to a group of Asian immigrant parents. The health educator is aware that English is a second language for many of the parents. Each of the following is a strategy that will help the educator overcome this language barrier in presenting information, EXCEPT   8._____

    A. speaking more loudly
    B. using images, gestures, and simple written instructions that may be understood by relatives
    C. speaking slowly and enunciating clearly
    D. repeating sentences in the same words if it's been misunderstood

9. A person who takes the structuralist view of behavior and social change will probably focus his or her efforts on the   9._____

    A. laws, codes, zoning ordinances, and taxation of the community
    B. sense of shared purpose among community members
    C. biomedical causes of a disease or disorder
    D. individual's motivation for change

10. When defining and organizing a written message for an adult audience with limited reading skills, a health educator's sentences should   10._____

    A. include vivid descriptive phrases to add interest
    B. average 8 to 10 words in length
    C. have roughly the same rhythm
    D. be written in the passive voice

11. In researching a community profile, most of the information can be obtained from the data collected by the   11._____

    A. local hospitals
    B. state and local social service departments
    C. chambers of commerce
    D. federal Bureau of the Census

12. When deciding whether to use visuals as part of health instruction, the primary consideration should be whether they   12.____

    A. enhance the message, rather than compete with it
    B. illustrate key concepts
    C. stimulate learner interest
    D. are culturally appropriate

13. The probability for learning in a health education program is likely to be enhanced when the following principles are used in program design: 13.____
    I. Program content is relevant to the learner, and is perceived by the learner to be relevant.
    II. Instructional methods that stimulate the widest variety of senses will generally be most effective.
    III. Concepts should be reviewed and repeated several times during instruction.
    IV. Instruction should move from the unknown to the known.

    A. I and IV
    B. I, II and III
    C. II and III
    D. I, II, III and IV

14. Which of the following is MOST likely to be a kind of formative evaluation used for a health education program?   14.____

    A. Studies of public behavior/health change
    B. Assessment of target audience for knowledge gain
    C. Calculation of percentage of target audience participating
    D. Focus group

15. In social marketing theory, the best example of a "channel gatekeeper" would be a   15.____

    A. mother of a large urban family
    B. postal carrier
    C. human resources manager at a large corporation
    D. social worker specializing in substance abuse

16. A health agency plans to publish its own nutrition handbook. Guidelines for the visual design of such a publication include   16.____
    I. Concepts that belong together or have similarities should be boxed in.
    II. Narrow columns, rather than full-page-wide text, should be used.
    III. When paragraphs are short, do not indent
    IV. If possible, margins should be wider at the bottom than at the top of the page.

    A. I only
    B. I and IV
    C. II and III
    D. I, II, III and IV

17. Which of the following is NOT a risk factor associated with cirrhosis?   17.____

    A. Infectious agents
    B. High blood cholesterol

    C.   Alcohol abuse
    D.   Biological factors

18.   Which of the following types of funding is MOST likely to be awarded for a program that   18._____
originates with the funding source?

    A.   Grant
    B.   Public funds
    C.   Private funds
    D.   Contract

19.   The PROCEED model of planning health education programs adds each of the following   19._____
procedures to the PRECEDE model, EXCEPT assessment of

    A.   budgetary and staff resources required
    B.   barriers to overcome in delivering health education
    C.   predisposing, enabling, and reinforcing factors among community members
    D.   policies that can be used to support the program

20.   Theatrical or dramatization exercises are sometimes a useful means of instruction in   20._____
health education. Generally, a disadvantage associated with this activity is that it

    A.   may make some participants uncomfortable
    B.   stimulates participants' emotions
    C.   distracts from the real purpose of the program
    D.   may make issues seem artificial or contrived

21.   Which of the following questions would be MOST likely to appear in the formative evalua-   21._____
tion of a health education program?

    A.   Did the media organizations that the agency contacted change their practices to
        include photos of safe bicycling?
    B.   How many agency-sponsored activities received coverage in the local press?
    C.   How many members actively monitored the local media on a regular basis?
    D.   How many parents were influenced to buy bicycle helmets after reading the
        agency's press releases?

22.   A health educator wants to draw attention to a new program by placing an op-ed piece   22._____
about AIDS awareness in the local newspaper. The ideal length for such a piece would
be about _____ words.

    A.   100
    B.   300
    C.   800
    D.   1200

23.   Of the following areas for change, most nationwide initiatives focusing on public health,   23._____
such as Healthy People 2000, place the highest priority on

    A.   alcohol and other drugs
    B.   nutrition
    C.   maternal and infant health
    D.   food and drug safety

24. Problems or shortcomings associated with the client-centered approach to health educa- 24.____
tion include:
    I.   Clients tend to overemphasize environmental determinants of health, such as socio-economic conditions and unemployment.
    II.   Clients' prior experience may have led them to need and want professional leadership.
    III.   Choices of materials and methods usually involve some sort of value judgement on the part of the health educator.
    IV.   There may be a conflict between the identified concerns of a client and those of the professional.

    A.   I and II
    B.   II and IV
    C.   III only
    D.   I, II, III and IV

25. In conducting a community assessment, advantages associated with focus group inter- 25.____
views include
    I.   potential use as a marketing tool
    II.   teaching and learning taking place on many levels
    III.   possible function as support group for some members
    IV.   increased likelihood of candid, unbiased assessments

    A.   In only
    B.   I, II and III
    C.   II and IV
    D.   I, II, III and IV

KEY (CORRECT ANSWERS)

1.	C		11.	D
2.	A		12.	A
3.	D		13.	B
4.	A		14.	D
5.	B		15.	C
6.	C		16.	D
7.	C		17.	B
8.	A		18.	D
9.	A		19.	C
10.	B		20.	A

21.	C
22.	C
23.	B
24.	B
25.	B

TEST 3

DIRECTIONS: Each question or incomplete statement is followed by several suggested answers or completions. Select the one the BEST answers the question or completes the statement. *PRINT THE LETTER OF THE CORRECT ANSWER IN THE SPACE AT THE RIGHT.*

1. From a health education perspective, the key to developing strategies for risk reduction in a community is/are the

    A. receptiveness of the community to intervention
    B. particular health risks generally associated with the community
    C. geographic and hygienic factors in the community
    D. shared values and institutions of the community

1.____

2. As a funding source for health education programs, foundations usually

    A. provide annual reports and funding guidelines on request
    B. provide gifts in kind
    C. don't specify what kind of projects will be funded
    D. don't fund projects requesting 100 percent funding

2.____

3. A health educator who takes a holistic approach to service delivery is probably more likely than traditional practitioners to make use of

    A. existing government structures and programs
    B. translators or community liaisons
    C. secondary health education
    D. natural support systems

3.____

4. A health agency has composed a 15-second public service announcement to be aired on local television. The agency wants to learn how and whether the announcement stands out among the clutter of other messages broadcast each day. Assuming adequate resources, the best possible pre-test for the PSA would be

    A. self-administered questionnaires
    B. focus groups
    C. theater testing
    D. individual interviews

4.____

5. At a bare minimum, a comprehensive health promotion program at a major worksite should include each of the following activities, EXCEPT

    A. group weight loss programs
    B. exercise and fitness programs
    C. nutrition counseling
    D. health risk appraisals

5.____

6. A health educator is in the process of recruiting workers at an automobile manufacturing plant for a wellness program. The educator should know that the most effective way to involve blue-collar workers in a worksite program is to avoid

6.____

A. one-on-one counseling or guided self-help
B. setting up screening stations where large numbers of employees work in the production area or the lunchroom, for example
C. a reliance on formal classes for reducing specific health risks
D. attempting to make any changes to the worksite itself

7. In sociology, the _____ theory suggests that society tends toward conservatism and maintenance of the status quo. 7._____

A. exchange
B. conflict
C. innovation-diffusion
D. consensus

8. When evaluating the success of a health education program, an agency should 8._____

A. coordinate the evaluation effort with all phases of the program and all levels of personnel
B. select the most thorough evaluation possible
C. opt for sophisticated and complex evaluation approaches
D. generally ignore subjective inputs from participants

9. Usually, the most effective and efficient way of overcoming a language barrier between a health educator and a group of clients is to 9._____

A. learn the client language in order to interact more personably with them
B. train and use bilingual community members for use in programs
C. provide a course in English "survival" skills for clients
D. seek the help of a health care professional who is fluent in the client language

10. A health educator plans to use headings as an organizational tool in her food safety brochure. Which of the following statements about the use of headings in printed material is generally FALSE? 10._____

A. For competent readers, headings are most effective when used with long paragraphs.
B. Visuals with headings allow readers to react before more detailed information is given.
C. One-word headings are more instructional and eye-catching than brief explanatory phrases.
D. Captions or headings should summarize and emphasize important information.

11. Of the following visual tools for instruction or promotion, which is generally LEAST likely to influence behavior change? 11._____

A. Flipchart
B. Poster
C. Talk board
D. Model

12. In planning a health education program, a group states the goals of its planning process briefly, and then lists in sequence all the steps or activities needed to accomplish the goals. Target data for program implementation is established, and a timetable for each phase of the process is developed. The best way to visually represent this process, in order to illustrate task interde-pendencies, is the

    A. PERT chart
    B. decision tree
    C. Gantt chart
    D. nomograph

12.____

13. Each of the following is an example of primary health education, EXCEPT a course in

    A. contraception
    B. quitting smoking
    C. personal relationships
    D. nutrition

13.____

14. A correlational study reveals a strong positive relationship between the amount of time subjects spend at their workplace and the incidence of obesity. One researcher, studying the data, raises the possibility that a tendency to spend long hours at work and obesity may both be the result of a certain slowing of the metabolic processes. This is known as

    A. bidirectional causation
    B. a longitudinal relationship
    C. the third-variable problem
    D. a multivariate analysis

14.____

15. The main problem or shortcoming associated with the social change approach to health education is the

    A. assumption that "experts" have the "right" answers to complex health problems
    B. political sensitivity of many health issues
    C. lack of community resources available to many clients to reduce health risks
    D. reliance on the value judgements of the health educator

15.____

16. When conducting a survey of the community at large, a health educator should

    A. select respondents based on their potential gain from proposed programs
    B. collect as large a sample as possible and use these data to make final program decisions
    C. consider it a way of increasing community awareness
    D. combine results with data obtained from community opinion leaders

16.____

17. Guidelines for the use of visuals as part of health instruction include
    I. Images of people in the visuals should look like members of the intended audience
    II. Illustrate both desired and undesired behaviors
    III. Avoid diagrams, graphs, and other complicated visuals
    IV. The number of visuals should be limited to emphasize the most important points

17.____

A. I only
B. I, III and IV
C. II and III
D. I, II, III and IV

18. Which of the following is a risk factor associated with diabetes?   18._____

A. Drug abuse
B. Obesity
C. Environmental factors
D. Stress

19. Which of the following questions would be MOST likely to appear in the summative eval-   19._____
uation of a health education program?

A. How often did staff and members meet with local media representatives to encourage coverage of the agency's breast-feeding classes?
B. How many times did the agency submit press releases or letters to the editor?
C. Which other members of the community besides the local press were notified
regarding the agency's breast-feeding classes?
D. How many mothers attended the breast-feeding classes that were offered by the
agency?

20. According to the PATCH model of health education planning developed by the Centers   20._____
for Disease Control and Prevention, the FIRST step in implementing a health education
program is

A. mobilizing the community
B. choosing health priorities
C. enhancement of community awareness about the program
D. developing a comprehensive intervention strategy

21. When making a comparison of mortality rates by race, sex, and age groups, a health   21._____
educator will need to aggregate _____ of data, unless the community is a large

A. 6 to 12 months
B. 12 to 18 months
C. 3 to 5 years
D. 5 to 10 years

22. A health educator is asked by the agency director to write a public service announce-   22._____
ment to be aired on the radio. The agency has purchased a 20-second spot. The PSA
should be about _____ words in length.

A. 20-25
B. 30-35
C. 40-50
D. 60-75

23. Professional standards for implementing health education programs at the local level   23._____
include each of the following principles and guidelines, EXCEPT

A. an emphasis on health outcomes
B. a fill-in-the-blanks approach to allow communities to establish objectives

C.   a focus on professional practice standards, rather than programs
D.   the importance of negotiating responsibilities between state and local agencies

24.   A health educator decides that in conducting a seminar for elderly Asian-American   24.____
women on the risk factors associated with osteoporosis, she will adopt a permissive
communication style. A potential disadvantage associated with this decision is that clients may

A.   conform to other people's ideas, rather than develop their own
B.   become fearful and reluctant to take independent action
C.   lose self-respect and motivation to change
D.   not receive important advice or information unless they ask for it

25.   As a mass media channel for the communication of a health-related message or public   25.____
service announcement, newspapers

A.   are most likely to reach audiences who do not typically use the health care system
B.   can be used to more specifically target segments of the public
C.   involve strict government regulation concerning the content of public service mes-
sages
D.   usually involve the most thorough coverage, but the smallest likelihood of audience
attention

—————

KEY (CORRECT ANSWERS)

1.	D		11.	B
2.	A		12.	A
3.	D		13.	B
4.	C		14.	C
5.	A		15.	B
6.	C		16.	C
7.	D		17.	B
8.	A		18.	B
9.	B		19.	D
10.	C		20.	A

21.	C
22.	C
23.	C
24.	D
25.	D

—————

EXAMINATION SECTION
TEST 1

DIRECTIONS: Each question or incomplete statement is followed by several suggested answers or completions. Select the one that BEST answers the question or completes the statement. *PRINT THE LETTER OF THE CORRECT ANSWER IN THE SPACE AT THE RIGHT.*

1. The community can influence the spread of disease or the collective health and well-being by   1._____

    A.   providing barriers to protect from health hazards
    B.   organizing ways to combat outbreaks of infection
    C.   promoting practices that contribute to individual and community health
    D.   all of the above

2. In community health practice, a *community* is defined PRIMARILY by   2._____

    A.   skin color
    B.   geography and common interest and health problems
    C.   age group
    D.   ethnic origin

3. *Health,* as defined by WHO, is a state   3._____

    A.   in which a person is strong, tough, and fat
    B.   in which a person is free from disease
    C.   of complete physical, mental, and social well-being and not merely the absence of disease or infirmity
    D.   none of the above

4. The CRITICAL element of community health practice which provides a means of solving problems and exploring new and improved methods of health service is   4._____

    A.   preventive health service
    B.   a health protection agency
    C.   research
    D.   polydevelopment

5. A social worker who discovers that a young mother has herself been a victim of child abuse, institutes early treatment for the mother to prevent abuse and foster adequate parenting of her children.
    This is an example of   5._____

    A.   health protection
    B.   preventive health service
    C.   health promotion
    D.   health assessment

6. The treatment of disorders, focusing on illness and health problems, aims to provide   6.____

    A. direct service to people with health problems
    B. indirect service by assisting people with health problems
    C. development of programs to correct unhealthy conditions
    D. all of the above

7. Community health nursing does NOT attempt to   7.____

    A. provide services in the contexts of family and community
    B. focus on cures, rather than preventive care
    C. serve clients of all ages
    D. enhance individual, family, and community group health

8. Community health nursing   8.____

    A. focuses on populations rather than individuals
    B. does not collaborate with other disciplines
    C. provides services only on a community basis
    D. addresses only primary levels of prevention

9. A nursing student asks you about community health nursing. You would include all of the   9.____
following characteristics EXCEPT:
It

    A. collaborates with other disciplines
    B. focuses on preventive rather than curative care
    C. addresses only tertiary levels of prevention
    D. does not encourage the client"s active and collaborative participation in health pro-
       motion activities

10. Community health nursing promotes a healthy lifestyle by doing all of the following   10.____
EXCEPT

    A. providing health education
    B. demonstrating healthy living skills
    C. prescribing drugs
    D. directing health care system efforts to provide the client with health promotion
       options

11. Among the INDIRECT services provided by a community health nurse is: 11.____

    A. Resource planning and development
    B. Health counseling for clients having potential or diagnosed disorders
    C. Health education regarding illness and wellness states
    D. Care for sick clients, including in-home nursing care

12. Community health nursing provides DIRECT services to ensure assistance for clients   12.____
with health problems, such as

    A. advocating new community health services
    B. participating in resource planning and development
    C. providing in-home nursing care
    D. developing programs to correct unhealthy community conditions

13. Community health nursing promotes rehabilitation by doing all of the following EXCEPT   13.____

    A. reducing client's disability
    B. occupational and physical therapy
    C. incorporating a group focus such as ostomy clubs, Alcoholics Anonymous, or half-way houses
    D. restoring client's function

14. Primary care services provided by community health nurses do NOT include   14.____

    A. providing health services that are the client's first contact with the health care system during any illness episode
    B. assuming responsibility for a continuum of care
    C. formulating community diagnoses
    D. providing services through the expanded role of nurse practitioner

15. All of the following are elements of community service provided by the community health nurse EXCEPT   15.____

    A. assuming responsibility for continuum of care
    B. formulating community diagnoses
    C. planning services that address community needs
    D. identifying community health problems

16. The one of the following which the American Nurses' Association does NOT define as a basic concept of community health nursing is the provision of   16.____

    A. synthesis of nursing and public health practices
    B. episodic care
    C. services to promote and preserve the health of populations
    D. general and comprehensive care

17. According to the American Nurses' Association, community health nursing focuses on all of the following EXCEPT   17.____

    A. health industry
    B. health promotion
    C. health education
    D. holistic management of client health care

18. Basic concepts of community health nursing, as defined by the American Public Health Association, include all of the following EXCEPT   18.____

    A. synthesizing public health sciences knowledge and professional nursing theories
    B. seeking to improve the health of the entire community
    C. only preventive measures
    D. multidisciplinary teams and programs

19. The FIRST people to recognize the need for trained nurses were the   19.____

    A. Romans   B. Greeks   C. Egyptians   D. Jews

20. The Hebrew hygienic code (c. 1500 B.C.) established a prototype for personal and community sanitation standards, including 20.____

    A. dietary omissions and food preparation guidelines
    B. personal cleanliness
    C. quarantine for individuals with communicable diseases
    D. all of the above

21. Through the Middle Ages, communicable disease epidemics, including cholera, leprosy, bubonic plague, and smallpox, were caused by 21.____

    A. poor personal hygiene
    B. excreta accumulation
    C. poor housing conditions
    D. all of the above

22. The voluntary nursing services provided to the poor and sick by charitable agencies during the 19th century were known as _____ nursing. 22.____

    A. public health   B. community health
    C. district   D. family practice

23. Medicare and Medicaid programs necessitated changes in nursing practice, including 23.____

    A. establishing home health care agencies as bases for community health nursing practice
    B. revising and standardizing nursing care procedures
    C. expanding nursing programs to include physical therapy, occupational therapy, etc.
    D. all of the above

24. The conceptual model, as used in community health nursing, is NOT a 24.____

    A. symbolic representation of reality
    B. schematic representation of some relationships between phenomena
    C. use of symbols or diagrams to represent an idea
    D. none of the above

25. Conceptual models used in community health nursing 25.____

    A. attempt to describe, explain, and sometimes predict the relationship between phenomena
    B. are composed of abstract and general concepts and propositions
    C. facilitate communications among nurses, and encourage a unified approach to practice, teaching, and research
    D. all of the above

KEY (CORRECT ANSWERS)

1.	D		11.	A
2.	B		12.	C
3.	C		13.	B
4.	C		14.	C
5.	D		15.	A
6.	D		16.	B
7.	B		17.	A
8.	A		18.	C
9.	D		19.	B
10.	C		20.	D

21.	D
22.	C
23.	D
24.	D
25.	D

————

TEST 2

DIRECTIONS: Each question or incomplete statement is followed by several suggested answers or completions. Select the one that BEST answers the question or completes the statement. *PRINT THE LETTER OF THE CORRECT ANSWER IN THE SPACE AT THE RIGHT.*

1. A set of interrelated concepts providing a systematic, explanatory and predictive view of a phenomenon is known as a

    A. concept   B. theory
    C. hypothesis   D. rule

1.____

2. All of the following are true for a theory EXCEPT that it

    A. can describe a particular phenomenon
    B. can explain relationships between phenomena
    C. is not logical
    D. can predict the effects of one phenomenon on another and be used to produce a desired phenomenon

2.____

3. Of the following, the INCORRECT statement regarding the symbolic interactionism theory is that it

    A. originated in the works of pragmatist philosophers William James, John Dewey, and George Herbert Mead
    B. used to study and conceptualize basic social processes
    C. applied specifically to individual study by nursing and other disciplines
    D. provides a means of understanding human interactive behavior

3.____

4. The symbolic interactionism theory

    A. focuses on how individuals define their situations and on the consequences of their actions
    B. emphasizes internal family dynamics
    C. analyzes how role definition and interactions develop and change over time
    D. all of the above

4.____

5. Internal family dynamics, emphasized by the symbolic interactionism theory, include all of the following EXCEPT:

    A. an individual's role definition
    B. an individual's interactions with others
    C. perception of the person's role within the family
    D. effect of the individual and family on the community

5.____

6. The MOST important community health nursing implication in the symbolic interactionism theory is to

    A. work within the client's role definition
    B. assess group dynamics affecting the client
    C. help the client self-assess actions and their consequences
    D. evaluate the client, family or community role definition and its effects on interactions

6.____

7. All of the following are major concepts of the system theory used in community health nursing EXCEPT: 7.____

    A. Systems are sets of organized components that react to and interact with other systems in their environment.
    B. Systems are both open and closed.
    C. A system reacts as a whole; the dysfunction of one system component affects the entire system.
    D. Systems employ a feedback cycle of input, throughput, and output.

8. According to the developmental theory used in community health nursing, the family   8.____

    A. is not a social system
    B. is not a task-performing unit
    C. does not have relatively open boundaries
    D. is not continually confronting and dealing with change

9. Regarding the use of the developmental theory in community health nursing, it is IMPORTANT to   9.____
    I. use knowledge of developmental tasks when assessing and implementing needed community services
    II. observe the family at home to accurately assess the developmental cycle
    III. anticipate family life cycle stages and provide appropriate family guidance in community settings
    IV. apply developmental framework to only non-traditional families
The CORRECT answer is:

    A. I, II, III   B. I, III, IV
    C. II, III, IV   D. II, IV

10. The MOST important major concept of the Roy adaptation model used in community health nursing is that   10.____

    A. people are adaptive systems
    B. stimuli, or input, cause system changes
    C. system changes may be adaptive or maladaptive to the system
    D. two mechanisms control the system: the cognator and the regulator

11. Which of the following modes does NOT affect or implement system adaptation?   11.____

    A. Self-concept   B. Role function
    C. Pathologic   D. Interdependence

12. The Roy Adaptation Model is NOT used   12.____

    A. as a framework for assessing the client and the family in the community environment
    B. as a basis for client education and health promotion planning
    C. to develop a comprehensive plan of care by assessing only one adaptive mode
    D. to try to maintain and maximize family modes of adaptation

13. All of the following are accurate characteristics of Rogers' science of unitary man EXCEPT: 13.____

    A. Developed in 1970 by nurse theorist Martha Rogers
    B. Based on behavior model systems
    C. Includes developmental model elements
    D. Based on general systems theory

14. The MAJOR concept of Rogers' science of unitary man is that   14.____

    A. self-care agency refers to a person's ability to perform self-care actions
    B. systems are open or closed
    C. individuals and their environments are viewed as energy fields characterized by wave patterns
    D. the family is a social system

15. Which of the following is a community health nursing implication of Rogers' science of unitary man?   15.____

    A. Individuals and their environments are viewed as energy fields characterized by wave patterns.
    B. Systems have four-dimensionality.
    C. To promote and maintain health, prevent disease, and diagnose and intervene in illnesses.
    D. All of the above.

16. Johnson's behavior systems model   16.____

    A. includes behavioral model subsystems
    B. is based on systems theory
    C. was developed in 1968 by nurse theorist Dorothy Johnson
    D. all of the above

17. Among the major concepts of Johnson's behavior systems model is the idea that the   17.____

    A. entire behavior system has functional requirements of protection, nurturing, and stimulation
    B. systems have four-dimensionality
    C. behavior system contains four subsystems, each of which have seven elements
    D. all of the above

18. All of the following are subsystems of the behavior system EXCEPT   18.____

    A. affiliation   B. achievement
    C. implementation   D. elimination

19. _____ is NOT an element of subsystems.   19.____

    A. Drive or goal   B. Predisposition to act
    C. Action alternatives   D. Ingestion

20. The entire behavior system, including subsystems, has functional requirements of all of the following EXCEPT   20.____

    A. protection   B. aggression
    C. nurturing   D. stimulation

21. Johnson's behavior systems model does NOT attempt to   21._____

    A. promote efficient and effective health-related behavior in human systems
    B. analyze the seven subsystems of a client's behavior as functional or dysfunctional
    C. help the client change ineffective responses to effective responses in the home environment
    D. direct and redirect client system and environmental patterns and organization

22. All of the following are major concepts of Orem's self-care model EXCEPT: 22._____

    A. A self-care deficit occurs when therapeutic self-care demand exceeds self-care agency.
    B. Dependent care agency refers to a person's ability to perform self-care actions.
    C. Systems exhibit patterns and organizations.
    D. Self-care denotes performing personal activities necessary to maintain life, health, and well-being.

23. Which of the following are community health nursing implications of Orem's self-care model?   23._____
    I. Implement nursing systems that are wholly compensatory, partially compensatory, or supportive-educative.
    II. Use these systems to meet the self-care needs of an individual, family, or community until self-care agency is restored.
    III. Examine universal, developmental, and health deviation self-care requisites when assessing community health needs.
    IV. Promote a harmonious interaction between the client and environment.
The CORRECT answer is:

    A. I, II, III   B. I, II, IV
    C. I, III, IV   D. II, III, IV

24. Neuman's systems model   24._____

    A. was developed in 1972 by nurse theorist Betty Neuman
    B. is characterized as an open systems model with two components; stress and stress reaction
    C. is based on Gestalt theory and psychology field theories
    D. all of the above

25. The MOST important concept of Neuman's systems model is that the   25._____

    A. core, or center, of the circles represents those things necessary for life
    B. individual is depicted by concentric circles with impacting stressors
    C. outer circle represents the flexible line of defense against stressors
    D. middle represents the normal line of defense

———

KEY (CORRECT ANSWERS)

1.	B		11.	C
2.	C		12.	C
3.	B		13.	B
4.	D		14.	C
5.	D		15.	D
6.	D		16.	D
7.	B		17.	A
8.	C		18.	C
9.	A		19.	D
10.	A		20.	B

21.	D
22.	C
23.	A
24.	D
25.	B

———

EXAMINATION SECTION

TEST 1

DIRECTIONS: Each question or incomplete statement is followed by several suggested answers or completions. Select the one that BEST answers the question or completes the statement. *PRINT THE LETTER OF THE CORRECT ANSWER IN THE SPACE AT THE RIGHT.*

1. Professional staff members in large organizations are sometimes frustrated by a lack of vital work-related information because of the failure of some middle-management supervisors to pass along unrestricted information from top management.
   All of the following are considered to be reasons for such failure to pass along information EXCEPT the supervisors'
   A. belief that information affecting procedures will be ignored unless they are present to supervise their subordinates
   B. fear that specific information will require explanation or justification
   C. inclination to regard the possession of information as a symbol of higher status
   D. tendency to treat information a private property

1.____

2. Increasingly in government, employees' records are being handled by automated data processing systems. However, employees frequently doubt a computer's ability to handle their records properly.
   Which of the following is the BEST way for management to overcome such doubts?
   A. Conduct a public relations campaign to explain the savings certain to result from the use of computers
   B. Use automated data processing equipment made by the firm which has the best repair facilities in the industry
   C. Maintain a clerical force to spot check on the accuracy of the computer's recordkeeping
   D. Establish automated data processing systems that are objective, impartial, and take into account individual factors as far as possible

2.____

3. Some management experts question the usefulness of offering cash to individual employees for their suggestions.
   Which of the following reasons for opposing cash awards is MOST valid?
   A. Emphasis on individual gain deters cooperative effort.
   B. Money spent on evaluating suggestions may outweigh the value of the suggestions.
   C. Awards encourage employees to think about unusual methods of doing work.
   D. Suggestions too technical for ordinary evaluation are usually presented.

3.____

4. The use of outside consultants, rather than regular staff, in studying and recommending improvements in the operations of public agencies has been criticized.
   Of the following, the BEST argument in favor of using regular staff is that such staff can better perform the work because they
   A. are more knowledgeable about operations and problems
   B. can more easily be organized into teams consisting of technical specialists
   C. may wish to gain additional professional experience
   D. will provide reports which will be more interesting to the public since they are more experienced

   4.____

5. One approach to organizational problem-solving is to have all problem-solving authority centralized at the top of the organization.
   However, from the viewpoint of providing maximum service to the public, this practice is UNWISE chiefly because it
   A. reduces the responsibility of the decision-makers
   B. produces delays
   C. reduces internal communications
   D. requires specialists

   5.____

6. Research has shown that problem-solving efficiency is optimal when the motivation of the problem-solver is at a moderate rather than an extreme level.
   Of the following, probably the CHIEF reason for this is that the problem-solver
   A. will cause confusion among his subordinates when his motivation is too high
   B. must avoid alternate solutions that tend to lead him up blind alleys
   C. can devote his attention to both the immediate problem as well as to other relevant problems in the general area
   D. must feel the need to solve the problem but not so urgently as to direct all his attention to the need and none to the means of solution

   6.____

7. Don't be afraid to make mistakes. Many organizations are paralyzed from the fear of making mistakes. As a result, they don't do the things they should; they don't try new and different ideas.
   For the effective supervisor, the MOST valid implication of this statement is that
   A. mistakes should not be encouraged, but there are some unavoidable risks in decision-making
   B. mistakes which stem from trying new and different ideas are usually not serious
   C. the possibility of doing things wrong is limited by one's organizational position
   D. the fear of making mistakes will prevent future errors

   7.____

8. The duties of an employee under your supervision may be either routine, problem-solving, innovative, or creative.
   Which of the following BEST describes duties which are both innovative and creative?

   8.____

A. Checking to make sure that work is done properly
B. Applying principles in a practical matter
C. Developing new and better methods of meeting goals
D. Working at two or more jobs at the same time

9. According to modern management theory, a supervisor who uses as little authority as possible and as much as is necessary would be considered to be using a mode that is

    A. autocratic   B. inappropriate
    C. participative   D. directive

9.____

10. Delegation involves establishing and maintaining effective working arrangements between a supervisor and the persons who report to him.
Delegation is MOST likely to have taken place when the
    A. entire staff openly discusses common problems in order to reach solutions satisfactory to the supervisor
    B. performance of specified work is entrusted to a capable person, and the expected results are mutually understood
    C. persons assigned to properly accomplish work are carefully evaluated and given a chance to explain shortcomings
    D. supervisor provides specific written instructions in order to prevent anxiety on the part of inexperienced persons

10.____

11. Supervisors often not aware of the effect that their behavior has on their subordinates.
The one of the following training methods which would be BEST for changing such supervisory behavior is _____ training.
    A. essential skills   B. off-the-job
    C. sensitivity   D. developmental

11.____

12. A supervisor, in his role as a trainer, may have to decide on the length and frequency of training sessions.
When the material to be taught is new, difficult, and lengthy, the trainer should be guided by the principle that for BEST results in such circumstances, sessions should be
    A. longer, relatively fewer in number, and held on successive days
    B. shorter, relatively greater in number, and spaced at intervals of several days
    C. of average length, relatively fewer in number, and held at intermittent intervals
    D. of random length and frequency, but spaced at fixed intervals

12.___

13. Employee training which is based on realistic simulation, sometimes known as *game play* or *role play*, is sometimes preferable to learning from actual experience on the job.
Which of the following is NOT a correct statement concerning the value of simulation to trainees?

13.____

A. Simulation allows for practice in decision-making without any need for subsequent discussion.
B. Simulation is intrinsically motivating because it offers a variety of challenges.
C. Compared to other, more traditional training techniques, simulation is dynamic.
D. The simulation environment is nonpunitive as compared to real life.

14. Programmed instruction as a method of training has all of the following advantages EXCEPT:　　14._____
　　A. Learning is accomplished in an optimum sequence of distinct steps.
　　B. Trainees have wide latitude in deciding what is to be learned within each program.
　　C. The trainee takes an active part in the learning process.
　　D. The trainee receives immediate knowledge of the results of his response.

15. In a work-study program, trainees were required to submit weekly written performance reports in order to insure that work assignments fulfilled the program objectives.　　15._____
Such reports would also assist the administrator of the work-study program PRIMARILY to
　　A. eliminate personal counseling for the trainees
　　B. identify problems requiring prompt resolution
　　C. reduce the amount of clerical work for all concerned
　　D. estimate the rate at which budgeted funds are being expended

16. Which of the following would be MOST useful in order to avoid misunderstanding when preparing correspondence or reports?　　16._____
　　A. Use vocabulary which is at an elementary level
　　B. Present each sentence as an individual paragraph
　　C. Have someone other than the writer read the material for clarity
　　D. Use general words which are open to interpretation

17. Which of the following supervisory methods would be MOST likely to train subordinates to give a prompt response to memoranda in an organizational setting where most transactions are informal?　　17._____
　　A. Issue a written directive setting forth a schedule of strict deadlines
　　B. Let it be known, informally, that those who respond promptly will be rewarded
　　C. Follow up each memorandum by a personal inquiry regarding the receiver's reaction to it
　　D. Direct subordinates to furnish a precise explanation for ignoring memos

18. Conferences may fail for a number of reasons. Still, a conference that is an apparent failure may have some benefit.　　18._____
Which of the following would LEAST likely be such a benefit?
It may
　　A. increase for most participants their possessiveness about information they have

B. produce a climate of good will and trust among many of the participants
C. provide most participants with an opportunity to learn things about the others
D. serve as a unifying force to keep most of the individuals functioning as a group

19. Assume that you have been assigned to study and suggest improvements in an operating unit of a delegate agency whose staff has become overwhelmed with problems, has had inadequate resources, and has become accustomed to things getting worse. The staff is indifferent to cooperating with you because they see no hope of improvement.
Which of the following steps would be LEAST useful in carrying out your assignment?
A. Encourage the entire staff to make suggestions to you for change
B. Inform the staff that management is somewhat dissatisfied with their performance
C. Let staff know that you are fully aware of their problems and stresses
D. Look for those problem area where changes can be made quickly

19.____

20. Which of the following statements about employer-employee relations is NOT considered to be correct by leading managerial experts?
A. An important factor in good employer-employee relations is treating workers respectfully.
B. Employer-employee relations are profoundly influenced by the fundamentals of human nature.
C. Good employer-employee relations must stem from top management and reach downward.
D. Employee unions are usually a major obstacle to establishing good employer-employee relations.

20.____

21. In connection with labor relations, the term *management rights* GENERALLY refers to
A. a managerial review system in a grievance system
B. statutory prohibitions that bar monetary negotiations
C. the impact of collective bargaining on government
D. those subjects which management considers to be non-negotiable

21.____

22. Barriers may exist to the utilization of women in higher level positions. Some of these barriers are attitudinal in nature.
Which of the following is MOST clearly attitudinal in nature?
A. Advancement opportunities which are vertical in nature and thus require seniority
B. Experience which is inadequate or irrelevant to the needs of a dynamic and progressive organization
C. Inadequate means of early identification of employees with talent and potential for advancement
D. Lack of self-confidence on the part of some women concerning their ability to handle a higher position

22.____

23. Because a reader reacts to the meaning he associates with a word, we can   23.____
neve be sure what emotional impact a word may carry or how it may affect our
readers.
The MOST logical implication of this statement for employees who correspond
with members of the public is that
   A. a writer should try to select a neutral word that will not bias his writing by
   its hidden emotional meaning
   B. simple language should be used in writing letters denying requests so
   that readers are not upset by the denial
   C. every writer should adopt a writing style which he finds natural and easy
   D. whenever there is doubt as to how a word is defined, the dictionary
   should be consulted

24. A public information program should be based on clear information about the   24.____
nature of actual public knowledge and opinion. One way of learning about the
views of the public is through the use of questionnaires.
Which of the following is of LEAST importance in designing a questionnaire?
   A. A respondent should be asked for his name and address.
   B. A respondent should be asked to choose from among several statements
   the one which expresses his views.
   C. Questions should ask for responses in a form suitable for processing.
   D. Questions should be stated in familiar language.

25. Assume that you have accepted an invitation to speak before an interested   25.____
group about a problem. You have brought with you for distribution a number of
booklets and other informational material.
Of the following, which would be the BEST way to use this material?
   A. Distribute it before you begin talking so that the audience may read it at
   their leisure.
   B. Distribute it during your talk to increase the likelihood that it will be read.
   C. Hold it until the end of your talk, then announce that those who wish may
   take or examine the material.
   D. Before starting the talk, leave it on a table in the back of the room so that
   people may pick it up as they enter.

————————

KEY (CORRECT ANSWERS)

1.	A	11.	C
2.	D	12.	B
3.	A	13.	A
4.	A	14.	B
5.	B	15.	B
6.	D	16.	C
7.	A	17.	C
8.	C	18.	A
9.	C	19.	B
10.	B	20.	D

21.	D
22.	D
23.	A
24.	A
25.	C

TEST 2

DIRECTIONS: Each question or incomplete statement is followed by several suggested answers or completions. Select the one that BEST answers the question or completes the statement. *PRINT THE LETTER OF THE CORRECT ANSWER IN THE SPACE AT THE RIGHT.*

1. Of the following, the FIRST step in planning an operation is to
   A. obtain relevant information
   B. identify the goal to be achieved
   C. consider possible alternatives
   D. make necessary assignments

   1.____

2. A supervisor who is extremely busy performing routine tasks is MOST likely making INCORRECT use of what basic principle of supervision?
   A. Homogeneous Assignment
   B. Span of Control
   C. Work Distribution
   D. Delegation of Authority

   2.____

3. Controls help supervisors to obtain information from which they can determine whether their staffs are achieving planned goals.
   Which one of the following would be LEAST useful as a control device?
   A. Employee diaries
   B. Organization charts
   C. Periodic inspections
   D. Progress charts

   3.____

4. A certain employee has difficulty in effectively performing a particular portion of his routine assignments, but his overall productivity is average.
   As the direct supervisor of his individual, your BEST course of action would be to
   A. attempt to develop the man's capacity to execute the problematic facets of his assignments
   B. diversify the employee's work assignments in order to build up his confidence
   C. reassign the man to less difficult tasks
   D. request in a private conversation that the employee improve his work output

   4.____

5. A supervisor who uses persuasion as a means of supervising a unit would GENERALLY also use which of the following practices to supervise his unit?
   A. Supervise and control the staff with an authoritative attitude to indicate that he is a *take-charge* individual
   B. Make significant changes in the organizational operations so as to improve job efficiency
   C. Remove major communication barriers between himself, subordinates, and management
   D. Supervise everyday operations while being mindful of the problems of his subordinates

   5.____

6. Whenever a supervisor in charge of a unit delegate a routine task to a capable subordinate, he tells him exactly how to do it.

   6.____

This practice is GENERALLY
- A. *desirable*, chiefly because good supervisors should be aware of the traits of their subordinates and delegate responsibilities to them accordingly
- B. *undesirable*, chiefly because only non-routine tasks should be delegated
- C. *desirable*, chiefly because a supervisor should frequently test the willingness of his subordinates to perform ordinary tasks
- D. *undesirable*, chiefly because a capable subordinate should usually be allowed to exercise his own discretion in doing a routine job

7. The one of the following activities through which a supervisor BEST demonstrates leadership ability is by
- A. arranging periodic staff meetings in order to keep his subordinates informed about professional developments in the field
- B. frequently issuing definite orders and directives which will lessen the need for subordinates to make decisions in handling any tasks assigned to them
- C. devoting the major part of his time to supervising subordinates so as to simulate continuous improvement
- D. setting aside time for self-development and research so as to improve the skills, techniques, and procedures of his unit

7._____

8. The following three statements relate to the supervision of employees:
- I. The assignment of difficult tasks that offer a challenge is more conducive to good morale than the assignment of easy tasks.
- II. The same general principles of supervision that apply to men are equally applicable to women.
- III. The best retraining program should cover all phases of an employee's work in a general manner.

Which of the following choices list ALL of the above statements that are generally correct?
- A. II, III
- B. I
- C. I, II
- D. I, II, III

8._____

9. Which of the following examples BEST illustrates the application of the *exception principle* as a supervisory technique?
- A. A complex job is divided among several employees who work simultaneously to complete the whole job in a shorter time.
- B. An employee is required to complete any task delegated to him to such an extent that nothing is left for the superior who delegated the task except to approve it.
- C. A superior delegates responsibility to a subordinate but retains authority to make the final decisions.
- D. A superior delegates all work possible to his subordinates and retains that which requires his personal attention or performance

9._____

10. Assume that you are a supervisor. Your immediate superior frequently gives orders to your subordinates without your knowledge.
Of the following, the MOST direct and effective way for you to handle this problem is to

10._____

    A. tell our subordinates to take orders only from you
    B. submit a report to higher authority in which you cite specific instances
    C. discuss it with your immediate superior
    D. find out to what extent your authority and prestige as a supervisor have been affected

11. In an agency which has as its primary purpose the protection of the public against fraudulent business practices, which of the following would GENERALLY be considered an *auxiliary* or *staff* rather than a *line* function?   11.____
    A. Interviewing victims of frauds and advising them about their legal remedies
    B. Daily activities directed toward prevention of fraudulent business practices
    C. Keeping records and statistics about business violations reported and corrected
    D. Follow-up inspections by investigators after corrective action has been taken

12. A supervisor can MOST effectively reduce the spread of false rumors through the *grapevine* by   12.____
    A. identifying and disciplining any subordinate responsible for initiating such rumors
    B. keeping his subordinates informed as much as possible about matters affecting them
    C. denying false rumors which might tend to lower staff morale and productivity
    D. making sure confidential matters are kept secure from access by unauthorized employees

13. A supervisor has tried to learn about the background, education, and family relationships of his subordinates through observation, personal contact, and inspection of their personnel records.
These supervisor actions are GENERALLY   13.____
    A. *inadvisable*, chiefly because they may lead to charges of favoritism
    B. *advisable*, chiefly because they may make him more popular with his subordinates
    C. *inadvisable*, chiefly because his efforts may be regarded as an invasion of privacy
    D. *advisable*, chiefly because the information may enable him to develop better understanding of each of his subordinates

14. In an emergency situation, when action must be taken immediately, it is BEST for the supervisor to give orders in the form of   14.____
    A. direct commands which are brief and precise
    B. requests, so that his subordinates will not become alarmed
    C. suggestions which offer alternative courses of action
    D. implied directives, so that his subordinates may use their judgment in carrying them out

15. When demonstrating a new and complex procedure to a group of subordinates, it is ESSENTIAL that a supervisor

    A. go slowly and repeat the steps involved at least once
    B. show the employees common errors and the consequences of such errors
    C. go through the process at the usual speed so that the employees can see the rate at which they should work
    D. distribute summaries of the procedure during the demonstration and instruct his subordinates to refer to them afterwards

15.____

16. After a procedures manual has been written and distributed,

    A. continuous maintenance work is necessary to keep the manual current
    B. it is best to issue new manuals rather than make changes in the original manual
    C. no changes should be necessary
    D. only major changes should be considered

16.____

17. Of the following, the MOST important criterion of effective report writing is

    A. eloquence of writing style
    B. the use of technical language
    C. to be brief and to the point
    D. to cover all details

17.____

18. The use of electronic data processing

    A. has proven unsuccessful in most organizations
    B. has unquestionable advantages for all organizations
    C. is unnecessary in most organizations
    D. should be decided upon only after careful feasibility studies by individual organizations

18.____

19. The PRIMARY purpose of work measurement is to

    A. design and install a wage incentive program
    B. determine who should be promoted
    C. establish a yardstick to determine extent of progress
    D. set up a spirit of competition among employee

19.____

20. The action which is MOST effective in gaining acceptance of a study by the agency which is being studied is

    A. a directive from the agency head to install a study based on recommendations included in a report
    B. a lecture-type presentation following approval of the procedure
    C. a written procedure in narrative form covering the proposed system with visual presentations and discussions
    D. procedural charts showing the *before* situation, forms, steps, etc., to the employees affected

20.____

21. Which organization principle is MOST closely related to procedural analysis and improvement?   21.____
    A. Duplication, overlapping, and conflict should be eliminated.
    B. Managerial authority should be clearly defined.
    C. The objectives of the organization should be clearly defined.
    D. Top management should be freed of burdensome detail.

22. Which one of the following is the MAJOR objective of operational audits?   22.____
    A. Detecting fraud
    B. Determining organization problems
    C. Determining the number of personnel needed
    D. Recommending opportunities for improving operating and management practices

23. Of the following, the formalization of organization structure is BEST achieved by   23.____
    A. a narrative description of the plan of organization
    B. functional charts
    C. job descriptions together with organization charts
    D. multi-flow charts

24. Budget planning is MOST useful when it achieves   24.____
    A. cost control   B. forecast of receipts
    C. performance review   D. personnel reduction

25. GENERALLY, in applying the principle of delegation in dealing with subordinates, a supervisor   25.____
    A. allows his subordinates to set up work goals and to fix the limits within which they can work
    B. allows his subordinates to set up work goals and then gives detailed orders as to how they are to be achieved
    C. makes relatively few decisions by himself and frames his orders in broad, general terms
    D. provides externalized motivation for his subordinate

KEY (CORRECT ANSWERS)

1.	B		11.	C
2.	D		12.	B
3.	B		13.	D
4.	A		14.	A
5.	D		15.	A
6.	D		16.	A
7.	C		17.	C
8.	C		18.	D
9.	D		19.	C
10.	C		20.	C

21.	A
22.	D
23.	C
24.	A
25.	C

EXAMINATION SECTION
TEST 1

DIRECTIONS: Each question or incomplete statement is followed by several suggested answers or completions. Select the one that BEST answers the question or completes the statement. *PRINT THE LETTER OF THE CORRECT ANSWER IN THE SPACE AT THE RIGHT.*

1. The aim of organization of a health department is to arrange people into working groups, associating those with similar functions or purposes in order to

    A. more efficiently obtain a desired result from group action
    B. provide proper channels for supervision
    C. assure staff development
    D. give the administrator a clear and concise picture of his staff

1.____

2. The goal of supervision in a nursing service is to

    A. see that the policies of the nursing service are carried out
    B. help nursing and ancillary personnel improve their skills and knowledge
    C. encourage the cooperation of nursing personnel so that the workload is evenly distributed
    D. improve nursing service to the community

2.____

3. Of the 21 critical objectives in the Healthy People 2010 initiative, which of the following is directly related to chronic disease prevention among adolescents and young adults?

    A. Reduce the proportion of children and adolescents who are overweight or obese
    B. Increase the proportion of adolescents who participate in daily school physical education
    C. Increase the proportion of school-based health centers with an oral health component
    D. Increase the proportion of schools that have a nurse-to-student ratio of at least 1:750

3.____

4. *Administratively,* the supervisor's PRINCIPAL function in a nursing service is to

    A. keep reliable schedules of nursing assignments and cases
    B. facilitate and further the service programs of the department
    C. screen problems for referral to administration
    D. consult with the health officer on administrative procedures

4.____

5. What piece of legislation requires Medicare-participating hospitals to establish and publicly report unit-by-unit staffing plans?

    A. Patient Protection and Affordable Care Act
    B. Registered Nurse Safe Staffing Act
    C. Medicare Modernization Act
    D. Social Security Act

5.____

6. The home visit is one of the most frequently used and highly regarded methods of pro-   6.____
viding service to the family.
The CHIEF advantage of the home visit over other methods is that it

    A. is less expensive and less time consuming than some group methods
    B. provides a better opportunity for the nurse to seek out new health problems
    C. permits the nurse to relate in a more meaningful way the experiences of other fam-
       ilies with similar problems which might be helpful in this situation
    D. permits the nurse to see the home and family in action for a more accurate
       appraisal of family relationships

7. When planning to visit a patient in her home for the first time, the nurse should be aware   7.____
that the PRIMARY purpose of a *first* visit is to

    A. gain information and build rapport
    B. analyze the health needs of the family
    C. teach the patient about her illness
    D. give information regarding available health facilities in the community

8. The supervised home visit as a method of professional guidance in nursing *ideally* MUST   8.____

    A. include a planning conference and an evaluation conference immediately after the
       visit
    B. provide for the supervisor's participation in nursing care during the visit
    C. allow opportunity for the supervisor to instruct the nurse during the visit
    D. be planned for a time when all members of the family are present

9. Of the following, the MOST advisable way for a supervising nurse to arrange for field vis-   9.____
its is to

    A. go when the nurse invites her to visit
    B. announce her visit without prior warning to the nurse
    C. plan the time and cases she will see with her staff
    D. plan her visits on a 6-month basis and post the schedule

10. The one of the following which is MOST essential in patient teaching by the nurse is the   10.____

    A. availability of health education literature in the health center
    B. provision for privacy during teaching conferences between supervisor and nurse
    C. maintenance of frequent contacts with the same patient
    D. nurse's ability to recognize teaching opportunities

11. Miss A., a nurse, told her supervisor that she felt that her visit to Mrs. Brown, who had   11.____
just returned home following a hysterectomy, was unproductive because she was unable
to teach Mrs. Brown the things she had planned for this visit. The supervisor asked the
nurse to briefly review her visit and, during the discussion, attempted to develop recognition of some positive accomplishments.
In this situation, the supervisor is practicing the principle of supervision which encour-
ages the nurse to

    A. practice critical analysis of an assignment
    B. make a self-evaluation of each planned visit
    C. gain some degree of security in the job
    D. make very definite plans for any home visit

12. The field visit is a valuable supervisory procedure, keeping the supervisor in close touch   12.____
with the realities of the work to be done.
In utilizing this procedure, the supervisor SHOULD

    A. be certain that the staff nurse fully accepts this method of supervision
    B. participate actively in the field visit as a method of reinforcing the cooperative rela-
tionship between supervisor and nurse
    C. concentrate upon observing every minute detail of the service which the nurse is
rendering
    D. precede the visit by careful preparation to help the nurse accept and utilize this
form of supervision

13. There is one school of thought in nursing supervision which believes that the supervised   13.____
home visit is not an appropriate supervisory method.
The MAIN reason underlying this conviction is that

    A. graduate nurses have been certified as competent by the schools which graduated
them
    B. the supervisor cannot know all the patient's problems in one visit
    C. the nurse-patient relationship is distorted by the introduction of a stranger
    D. there are more economic methods of supervision available

14. A planned orientation program is essential for the introduction of the new staff nurse to   14.____
the job.
In order for this orientation to be as efficient and economical as possible, it should have
for its *primary* goal the

    A. adjustment of the nurse to her new job and environment
    B. rapid absorption of the nurse into the service
    C. training of the nurse in the techniques essential for job performance
    D. elimination of certain inhibiting factors which the new nurse brings with her to the
job

15. The training period for newly-appointed nurses should   15.____

    A. include the same content for all newly employed staff
    B. vary according to previous experience
    C. be planned so that it can be completed within the period of probation
    D. be developed around individual supervisory conferences

16. The assignment of cases during the preliminary period is an important aspect of the   16.____
induction of a new worker.
Of the following, the statement which provides the BEST guide for the assignment of
cases to a new nurse is that

    A. every attempt should be made to provide the experience of handling every possible
type of case during this period
    B. her case load should be kept very light during this period in order to allow the new
worker to become adjusted to the work
    C. cases should be selected with the idea of providing this nurse with an opportunity
to try out her relationships with families and to see the function of the nurse in providing continuity of care
    D. cases should be selected that will hold her interest and provide a challenge to her

17. Continuing staff education activities as a responsibility of a nursing service are *neces-sary* CHIEFLY because   17._____

    A. only about one-third of the nurses have adequate training
    B. quality of service is closely related to staff development
    C. shared staff experiences help in the development of the individual nurse
    D. present-day case loads are too heavy to allow the nurse to plan her own continued education

18. The *objectives* of the on-going education program in a nursing service should be estab-lished   18._____

    A. on the basis of the previous experience records of staff
    B. in conference, by the director and supervisors
    C. cooperatively by all of the staff
    D. by the public health nurse section of the local professional nursing organization

19. The one of the following which is NOT characteristic of workshop activities is that the   19._____

    A. direction of the discussion and the activities are planned and carried out by the group
    B. experiences and knowledge of the group itself are used in defining and solving problems
    C. procedures are organized around problems presented by the participants
    D. procedures are organized around the formal presentation of a body of subject matter

20. The PRIMARY purpose of keeping records in nursing is to   20._____

    A. provide a basis for studying the service given by the agency in terms of meeting community health needs
    B. provide better health care to patients and families in the community
    C. furnish information for collection of epidemiological data
    D. assist in the evaluation of a nurse's performance in the field

21. Process recording has been recommended as a supervisory method for the introduction of new staff nurses and field students.
One DISADVANTAGE of the method is that the   21._____

    A. supervisor is unable to observe the complete situation including, particularly, the skills, tone of voice, and mannerisms of the nurse
    B. effectiveness of the record is minimized because it is a verbatim account rather than a summary of the visit
    C. procedure is too time-consuming to produce effective advantages for improving performance in interviewing and in enriching the teaching content of visits
    D. motivation for continuous self-evaluation by the nurse is lessened

22. Of the following, the one that represents the BEST basis for planning the content of a successful staff development program is the   22._____

    A. time available for meetings
    B. chief health problems of the community

C. common needs of the nurses as related to the situations with which they are deal-
    ing
D. experimental programs conducted by other agencies

23. Assume that a newly assigned supervising nurse calls her first staff conference with the   23.____
    nurses under her supervision.
    Of the following, the BEST approach to the group in this *initial* conference is for the
    supervisor

    A. after greeting the group, to explain that she will be making some changes in the
        method of supervision and in the schedules and to express her confidence that
        each nurse will cooperate with her as changes occur
    B. to learn from the group common practices and procedures and ways of relating to
        the previous supervisor and to assure them that only as the supervisor and nurses
        get to know each other better will any changes or essential adjustments be made if
        necessary
    C. to make use of this initial meeting for a brief, friendly introduction on a social rather
        than a business level and to postpone any questions or comments from the group
        until a subsequent meeting
    D. to encourage each nurse to talk freely about herself and any problems around her
        work in order to ascertain similarities or differences among the group members as
        a focus for supervision

24. Assume that you have arranged an individual conference with one of your staff nurses to   24.____
    discuss problems she has encountered in one of her cases.
    The one of the following on which it is MOST desirable for the supervisor to focus is the

    A. handling of the case in terms of departmental procedures
    B. nurse in terms of her educational background
    C. potential resources
    D. patient's problems in terms of his needs

25. The individual conference between nurse and supervisor has great potential for staff   25.____
    guidance and teaching. In planning for an individual conference with a nurse, the FUN-
    DAMENTAL concept that should guide all conference procedures is that

    A. the conference should provide an opportunity for staff and supervisor to discuss
        problems important to both and together to develop greater capacity to meet future
        problems
    B. the supervisor should keep control of the individual conference at all times in order
        to insure adequate time for covering the fundamental problems of the nurse
    C. the supervisor should subordinate all of her own thinking to that of the staff nurse
        so that the nurse can develop proper insight and initiative for future occasions
    D. it is important to allow sufficient time for the conference in order to permit establish-
        ing of cooperative relationships

KEY (CORRECT ANSWERS)

1.	A		11.	C
2.	D		12.	D
3.	A		13.	C
4.	B		14.	A
5.	B		15.	B
6.	D		16.	C
7.	A		17.	B
8.	A		18.	C
9.	C		19.	D
10.	D		20.	B

21.	A
22.	C
23.	B
24.	D
25.	A

———

TEST 2

DIRECTIONS: Each question or incomplete statement is followed by several suggested answers or completions. Select the one that BEST answers the question or completes the statement. *PRINT THE LETTER OF THE CORRECT ANSWER IN THE SPACE AT THE RIGHT.*

1. Suppose that one of your experienced nurses who has been carrying an assignment that requires great skill is leaving.
   Of the following, the LEAST appropriate way to select a replacement for this assignment is to

   A. ask the more skilled members of your staff individually if they are interested in this assignment
   B. review the educational backgrounds of present staff members
   C. consider the work performance of the present staff
   D. ask the staff group in conference for a volunteer for this assignment

   1.____

2. A graduate student assigned to work with you asks to be excused for two days for personal reasons and states she will make up the time before the end of her assignment. As the supervisor, it would be MOST advisable for you to

   A. grant this request as it seems reasonable
   B. advise the student to ask her faculty instructor to speak to you about this request
   C. refuse this request since it will interfere with the schedule of work
   D. question the student to see if her request is justified

   2.____

3. Assume that you have noticed that one of the nurses under your supervision avoids making antepartal visits whenever possible. During field observation of this nurse on an antepartal visit, you found it to be quite superficial, and in your conference with her, she admits that she feels inadequate on such visits.
   Of the following, the LEAST helpful action for you to take in this situation is to

   A. assign several more antepartal cases for her to visit without supervision
   B. suggest that she take a course on the subject at one of the local universities
   C. give her some selected readings on the subject
   D. plan to observe her more frequently on such cases

   3.____

4. A new nurse recently assigned to your office asks you whether it is better to write records in the patient's home or in the office.
   Of the following, the LEAST desirable statement for you to make to the nurse in your discussion with her is that

   A. all records, to be accurate, must be written in the patient's home
   B. case material which requires some organization and thought may better be written away from the home
   C. the nurse should rely upon her own judgment as to which place is better adapted to the recording of the type of information she must have for her records
   D. recording of certain information in the home, such as temperature or symptoms of illness, would seem to be necessary

   4.____

5. Suppose that a written directive has been received initiating a new policy on visits to   5.____
   adults in need of rehabilitation nursing.
   The FIRST thing that the supervisor should do in this situation is to

   A. issue a memorandum to the staff describing the new policy
   B. arrange for a staff conference to discuss the new policy
   C. plan a detailed education program to teach the staff how to make such visits
   D. arrange for observation by her staff of rehabilitation nursing in another agency

6. A nurse formerly in your office who resigned recently to return to school calls you to   6.____
   request that she be allowed to review some records to get material for a term paper.
   Of the following, the BEST action for you to take, since you are not sure of the department's policy on this type of request, is to

   A. plan an appropriate time for her to come in for this review since she is a former
      staff member known to your office
   B. explain that this is not possible because all records are confidential
   C. secure as much information as possible from her and explain that you will call her
      back after discussing her request with administration
   D. question her about the details of the paper and, if it seems worthwhile, grant her
      request

7. One of the nurses under your supervision tells you she is having some difficulty with her   7.____
   husband.
   Of the following, the MOST appropriate action for you to take is to

   A. listen sympathetically but make no comments
   B. suggest possible ways for the nurse to solve her problem
   C. explore the problem with the nurse to see if she can resolve it for herself
   D. discourage her from discussing the problem with you but suggest sources of help

8. You find that an increasing number of your staff are not following a certain procedure as   8.____
   directed in the manual.
   Of the following, the BEST course of action for you to take is to

   A. plan a group conference to explain that you want them to follow the set procedure
      at all times
   B. arrange a group conference and discuss this with your staff in order to learn why
      procedure is not being followed
   C. discuss this with each nurse who is not following procedure and explain that she
      must follow the instructions in the manual
   D. issue a written directive advising all nurses to consult their manuals on this matter

9. Routine checking of records by the supervisor is advisable CHIEFLY in order to   9.____

   A. maintain standards of service
   B. keep the supervisor and, through her, the director informed of services rendered to
      the community
   C. evaluate the performance of individual nurses on an objective basis
   D. reduce the cost of service to the community

10. When evaluating personnel, it is ESSENTIAL that individual differences be understood   10.____
    and accepted by both the individual employee and the supervisor so that the evaluation

A. does not result in a feeling of frustration for the employee
B. makes the individual who is being rated aware that she has shortcomings
C. can be used as a yardstick for appraising the work of the entire staff
D. results in acceptance by the employee of all of the supervisor's suggestions

11. Assume that during your observation of a nurse in the field she asks you for an evaluation of her work, which you feel was not as good as you had expecte
Of the following, the BEST action for you to take is to

A. discuss the visit with her immediately, frankly and in detail
B. avoid any discussion of the situation or visit by guiding conversation away from the subject
C. tell her that her work indicated both strengths and weaknesses but that you would like to discuss the details later in the office
D. tell her you would rather not discuss the visit with her until after you have reviewed the case record in the office

11._____

12. Present-day managerial practices advocate that adequate biographical levels of communication be maintained among all levels of nursing management.
Of the following, the BEST way to accomplish this is with

A. interdepartmental memoranda *only*
B. intradepartmental memoranda *only*
C. periodic staff meetings, interdepartmental and intradepartmental memoranda
D. interdepartmental and intradepartmental memoranda

12._____

13. It is generally agreed upon that it is important to have effective communications in the
nursing unit so that everyone knows exactly what is expected of him.
Of the following, the communications system which can assist in fulfilling this objective
BEST is one which consists of

A. written policies and procedures for administrative functions and verbal policies and procedures for professional functions
B. written policies and procedures for professional and administrative functions
C. verbal policies and procedures for professional and administrative functions
D. verbal policies and procedures for professional functions

13._____

14. If a head nurse wishes to build an effective department, she, *most generally*, must

A. be able to hire and fire as she feels necessary
B. consider the total aspects of her job, her influence and the effects of her decisions
C. have access to reasonable amounts of personnel and money with which to build her programs
D. attend as many professional conferences as possible so that she can keep up to date with all the latest advances in the field

14._____

15. Of the following, the factor which generally contributes MOST effectively to the performance of the nursing unit is that the senior nurse

A. personally inspect the work of all employees
B. service clients at a faster rate than her subordinates
C. have an exact knowledge of formulary
D. implement a program of professional development for her staff

15._____

103

16. Nursing workload reports compare workload to   16.____

    A. available professional time   B. number of patients served
    C. nurses' time devoted to it   D. nursing personnel budget

17. Administrative policies relate MOST closely to   17.____

    A. control of commodities and personnel
    B. general policies emanating from the nursing office
    C. fiscal management of the department *only*
    D. handling and dispensing of drugs

18. Part of being a good supervisor is to be able to develop an attitude towards employees   18.____
    which will motivate them to do their best on the jo
    The *good* nurse-supervisor, therefore, should

    A. take an interest in subordinates, but not develop an all-consuming attitude in this
       area
    B. remain in an aloof position when dealing with employees
    C. be as close to subordinates as possible on the job
    D. take a complete interest in all the activities of subordinates, both on and off the job

19. The practice of a supervisor assigning an experienced nurse to train new nurses instead   19.____
    of training them herself is generally considered

    A. *undesirable;* the more experienced nurse will resent being taken away from her
       regular job
    B. *desirable;* the supervisor can then devote more time to her regular duties
    C. *undesirable;* the more experienced nurse is not working at the proper level to train
       new employees
    D. *desirable;* the more experienced nurse is probably a better trainer than the supervi-
       sor

20. It is generally agreed that on-the-job training is MOST effective when new nurses are   20.____

    A. provided with study manuals, standard operating procedures, and other written
       materials to be studied for at least two weeks before the nurses attempt to do the
       job
    B. shown how to do the job in detail, and then instructed to do the work under close
       supervision
    C. trained by an experienced nurse for at least a week to make certain that the new
       nurses can do the job
    D. given work immediately which is checked at the end of each day

21. Nurses sometimes form small informal groups, commonly called cliques.   21.____
    With regard to the effect of such groups on processing of the workload, the attitude a
    supervisor should take towards these cliques is that of

    A. *acceptance,* since they take the nurses' minds off their work without wasting too
       much time
    B. *rejection,* since those nurses inside the clique tend to do less work than the outsid-
       ers
    C. *acceptance,* since the supervisor is usually included in the clique
    D. *rejection,* since they are usually disliked by higher management

22. Of the following, the BEST statement regarding rules and regulations in a nursing unit is that they   22.____

    A. are *necessary evils* to be tolerated by those at and above the first supervisory level only
    B. are stated in broad, indefinite terms so as to allow maximum amount of leeway in complying with them
    C. must be understood by all nurses in the unit
    D. are primarily for management's needs since insurance regulations mandate them

23. It is sometimes considered desirable for a nursing supervisor to survey the opinions of her nurses before taking action on decisions affecting them.
Of the following, the greatest DISADVANTAGE of following this approach is that the nurses might   23.____

    A. use this opportunity to complain rather than to make constructive suggestions
    B. lose respect for their supervisor whom they feel cannot make her own decisions
    C. regard this as an attempt by the supervisor to get ideas for which she can later claim credit
    D. be resentful if their suggestions are not adopted

24. Of the following, the MOST important reason for keeping statements of duties of nursing employees up to date is to   24.____

    A. serve as a basis of information for other governmental jurisdictions
    B. enable the department of personnel to develop job-related examinations
    C. differentiate between levels within the nursing occupational group
    D. enable each nursing employee to know what her duties are

25. Of the following, the BEST way to evaluate the progress of a new subordinate is to   25.____

    A. compare the output of the new nurse from week to week as to quantity and quality
    B. obtain the opinions of the new nurse's co-workers
    C. test the new nurse periodically to see how much she has learned
    D. hold frequent discussions with the nurse, focusing on her work

---

KEY (CORRECT ANSWERS)

1.	D		11.	C
2.	B		12.	C
3.	A		13.	B
4.	A		14.	B
5.	B		15.	D
6.	C		16.	A
7.	D		17.	A
8.	B		18.	A
9.	A		19.	B
10.	A		20.	B

21.   A
22.   C
23.   D
24.   D
25.   A

———

EXAMINATION SECTION
TEST 1

DIRECTIONS: Each question or incomplete statement is followed by several suggested answers or completions. Select the one that BEST answers the question or completes the statement. *PRINT THE LETTER OF THE CORRECT ANSWER IN THE SPACE AT THE RIGHT.*

1. In public agencies, communications should be based PRIMARILY on a   1._____
   A. two-way flow from the top down and from the bottom up, most of which should be given in writing to avoid ambiguity
   B. multi-direction flow among all levels and with outside persons
   C. rapid, internal one-way flow from the top down
   D. two-way flow of information, most of which should be given orally for purposes of clarity

2. In some organizations, changes in policy or procedures are often communicated   2._____
   by word of mouth from supervisors to employees with no prior discussion or exchange of viewpoints with employees.
   This procedure often produces employee dissatisfaction CHIEFLY because
   A. information is mostly unusable since a considerable amount of time is required to transmit information
   B. lower-level supervisors tend to be excessively concerned with minor details
   C. management has failed to seek employees' advice before making changes
   D. valuable staff time is lost between decision-making and the implementation of decisions

3. For good letter writing, you should try to visualize the person to whom you are   3._____
   writing, especially if you know him.
   Of the following rules, it is LEAST helpful in such visualization to think of
   A. the person's likes and dislikes, his concerns, and his needs
   B. what you would be likely to say if speaking in person
   C. what you would expect to be asked if speaking in person
   D. your official position in order to be certain that your words are proper

4. One approach to good informal letter writing is to make letters and   4._____
   conversational.
   All of the following practices will usually help to do this EXCEPT:
   A. If possible, use a style which is similar to the style used when speaking
   B. Substitute phrases for single words (e.g., *at the present time for now*)
   C. Use contractions of words (e.g., *you're* for *you are*)
   D. Use ordinary vocabulary when possible

5.   All of the following rules will aid in producing clarity in report-writing EXCEPT: 5.____
      A. Give specific details or examples, if possible
      B. Keep related words close together in each sentence
      C. Present information in sequential order
      D. Put several thoughts or ideas in each paragraph

6.   The one of the following statements about public relations which is MOST   6.____
     accurate is that
      A. in the long run, appearance gains better results than performance
      B. objectivity is decreased if outside public relations consultants are
           employed
      C. public relations is the responsibility of every employee
      D. public relations should be based on a formal publicity program

7.   The form of communication which is usually considered to be MOST personally   7.____
     directed to the intended recipient is the
      A. brochure   B. film   C. letter   D. radio

8.   In general, a document that presents an organization's views or opinions   8.____
     on a particular topic is MOST accurately known as a
      A. tear sheet   B. position paper
      C. flyer   D. journal

9.   Assume that you have been asked to speak before an organization of persons   9.____
     who oppose a newly announced program in which you are involved. You feel
     tense about talking to this group.
     Which of the following rules generally would be MOST useful in gaining rapport
     when speaking before the audience?
      A. Impress them with your experience
      B. Stress all areas of disagreement
      C. Talk to the group as to one person
      D. Use formal grammar and language

10. An organization must have an effective public relations program since, at its   10.____
     best, public relations is a bridge to change.
     All of the following statements about communication and human behavior have
     validity EXCEPT:
      A. People are more likely to talk about controversial matters with like-minded
           people than with those holding other views
      B. The earlier an experience, the more powerful its effect since it influences
           how later experiences will be interpreted
      C. In periods of social tension, official sources gain increased believability
      D. Those who are already interested in a topic are the ones who are most
           open to receive new communications about it

11. An employee should be encouraged to talk easily and frankly when he is   11.____
    dealing with his supervisor.
    In order to encourage such free communication, it would be MOST appropriate
    for a supervisor to behave in a(n)
    A. sincere manner; assure the employee that you will deal with him honestly
       and openly
    B. official manner; you are a supervisor and must always act formally with
       subordinates
    C. investigative manner; you must probe and question to get to a basis of
       trust
    D. unemotional manner; the employee's emotions and background should
       play no part in your dealings with him

12. Research findings show that an increase in free communication within an   12.____
    agency GENERALLY results in which one of the following?
    A. Improved morale and productivity
    B. Increased promotional opportunities
    C. An increase in authority
    D. A spirit of honesty

13. Assume that you are a supervisor and your superiors have given you a new-type   13.____
    procedure to be followed.
    Before passing this information on to your subordinates, the one of the
    following actions that you should take FIRST is to
    A. ask your superiors to send out a memorandum to the entire staff
    B. clarify the procedure in your own mind
    C. set up a training course to provide instruction on the new procedure
    D. write a memorandum to your subordinates

14. Communication is necessary for an organization to be effective.   14.____
    The one of the following which is LEAST important for most communication
    systems is that
    A. messages are sent quickly and directly to the person who needs them to
       operate
    B. information should be conveyed understandably and accurately
    C. the method used to transmit information should be kept secret so that
       security can be maintained
    D. senders of messages must know how their messages are received and
       acted upon

15. Which one of the following is the CHIEF advantage of listening willingly to   15.____
    subordinates and encouraging them to talk freely and honestly?
    It
    A. reveals to supervisors the degree to which ideas that are passed down
       are accepted by subordinates
    B. reduces the participation of subordinates in the operation of the
       department
    C. encourages subordinates to try for promotion
    D. enables supervisors to learn more readily what the *grapevine* is saying

16. A supervisor may be informed through either oral or written reports.   16._____
    Which one of the following is an ADVANTAGE of using oral reports?
    A. There is no need for a formal record of the report.
    B. An exact duplicate of the report is not easily transmitted to others.
    C. A good oral report requires little time for preparation.
    D. An oral report involves two-way communication between a subordinate
       and his supervisor.

17. Of the following, the MOST important reason why supervisors should   17._____
    communicate effectively with the public is to
    A. improve the public's understanding of information that is important for
       them to know
    B. establish a friendly relationship
    C. obtain information about the kinds of people who come to the agency
    D. convince the public that services are adequate

18. Supervisors should generally NOT use phrases like *too hard*, *too easy*, and   18._____
    a lot PRINCIPALLY because such phrases
    A. may be offensive to some minority groups
    B. are too informal
    C. mean different things to different people
    D. are difficult to remember

19. The ability to communicate clearly and concisely is an important element in   19._____
    effective leadership.
    Which of the following statements about oral and written communication is
    GENERALLY true?
    A. Oral communication is more time-consuming.
    B. Written communication is more likely to be misinterpreted.
    C. Oral communication is useful only in emergencies.
    D. Written communication is useful mainly when giving information to fewer
       than twenty people.

20. Rumors can often have harmful and disruptive effects on an organization.   20._____
    Which one of the following is the BEST way to prevent rumors from becoming a
    problem?
    A. Refuse to act on rumors, thereby making them less believable.
    B. Increase the amount of information passed along by the *grapevine*.
    C. Distribute as much factual information as possible.
    D. Provide training in report writing.

21. Suppose that a subordinate asks you about a rumor he has heard. The rumor   21._____
    deals with a subject which your superiors consider *confidential*.
    Which of the following BEST describes how you should answer the
    subordinate? Tell

    A. the subordinate that you don't make the rules and that he should speak to higher ranking officials
    B. the subordinate that you will ask your superior for information
    C. him only that you cannot comment on the matter
    D. him the rumor is not true

22. Supervisors often find it difficult to *get their message across* when instructing newly appointed employees in their various duties.
The MAIN reason for this is generally that the
    A. duties of the employees have increased
    B. supervisor is often so expert in his area that he fails to see it from the learner's point of view
    C. supervisor adapts his instruction to the slowest learner in the group
    D. new employees are younger, less concerned with job security and more interested in fringe benefits

22.____

23. Assume that you are discussing a job problem with an employee under your supervision. During the discussion, you see that the man's eyes are turning away from you and that he is not paying attention.
In order to get the man's attention, you should FIRST
    A. ask him to look you in the eye   B. talk to him about sports
    C. tell him he is being very rude   D. change your tone of voice

23.____

24. As a supervisor, you may find it necessary to conduct meetings with your subordinates.
Of the following, which would be MOST helpful in assuring that a meeting accomplishes the purpose for which it was called?
    A. Give notice of the conclusions you would like to reach at the start of the meeting.
    B. Delay the start of the meeting until everyone is present.
    C. Write down points to be discussed in proper sequence.
    D. Make sure everyone is clear on whatever conclusions have been reached and on what must be done after the meeting.

24.____

25. Every supervisor will occasionally be called upon to deliver a reprimand to a subordinate. If done properly, this can greatly help an employee improve his performance.
Which one of the following is NOT a good practice to follow when giving a reprimand?
    A. Maintain your composure and temper
    B. Reprimand a subordinate in the presence of other employees so they can learn the same lesson
    C. Try to understand why the employee was not able to perform satisfactorily
    D. Let your knowledge of the man involved determine the exact nature of the reprimand

25.____

―――――――

KEY (CORRECT ANSWERS)

1.	C		11.	A
2.	B		12.	A
3.	D		13.	B
4.	B		14.	C
5.	D		15.	A
6.	C		16.	D
7.	C		17.	A
8.	B		18.	C
9.	C		19.	B
10.	C		20.	C

21.	B
22.	B
23.	D
24.	D
25.	B

TEST 2

DIRECTIONS: Each question or incomplete statement is followed by several suggested answers or completions. Select the one that BEST answers the question or completes the statement. *PRINT THE LETTER OF THE CORRECT ANSWER IN THE SPACE AT THE RIGHT.*

1. Usually one thinks of communication as a single step, essentially that of transmitting an idea.
    Actually, however, this is only part of a total process, the FIRST step of which should be
    A. the prompt dissemination of the idea to those who may be affected by it
    B. motivating those affected to take the required action
    C. clarifying the idea in one's own mind
    D. deciding to whom the idea is to be communicated

1.____

2. Research studies on patterns of informal communication have concluded that most individuals in a group tend to be passive recipients of news, while a few make it their business to spread it around in an organization.
    With this conclusion in mind, it would be MOST correct for the supervisor to attempt to identify these few individuals and
    A. give them the complete facts on important matters in advance of others
    B. inform the other subordinates of the identity of these few individuals so that their influence may be minimized
    C. keep them straight on the facts on important matters
    D. warn them to cease passing along any information to others

2.____

3. The one of the following which is the PRINCIPAL advantage of making an oral report is that it
    A. affords an immediate opportunity for two-way communication between the subordinate and superior
    B. is an easy method for the superior to use in transmitting information to others of equal rank
    C. saves the time of all concerned
    D. permits more precise pinpointing of praise or blame by means of follow-up questions by the superior

3.____

4. An agency may sometimes undertake a public relations program of a defensive nature.
    With reference to the use of defensive public relations, it would be MOST correct to state that it
    A. is bound to be ineffective since defensive statements, even though supported by factual data, can never hope to even partly overcome the effects of prior unfavorable attacks
    B. proves that the agency has failed to establish good relationships with newspapers, radio stations, or other means of publicity

4.____

C. shows that the upper echelons of the agency have failed to develop sound public relations procedures and techniques
D. is sometimes required to aid morale by protecting the agency from unjustified criticism and misunderstanding of policies or procedures

5. Of the following factors which contribute to possible undesirable public attitudes towards an agency, the one which is MOST susceptible to being changed by the efforts of the individual employee in an organization is that   5._____
    A. enforcement of unpopular regulations as offended many individuals
    B. the organization itself has an unsatisfactory reputation
    C. the public is not interested in agency matters
    D. there are many errors in judgment committed by individual subordinates

6. It is not enough for an agency's services to be of a high quality; attention must also be given to the acceptability of these services to the general public.   6._____
   This statement is GENERALLY
    A. *false*; a superior quality of service automatically wins public support
    B. *true*; the agency cannot generally progress beyond the understanding and support of the public
    C. *false*; the acceptance by the public of agency services determines their quality
    D. *true*; the agency is generally unable to engage in any effective enforcement activity without public support

7. Sustained agency participation in a program sponsored by a community organization is MOST justified when   7._____
    A. the achievement of agency objectives in some area depends partly on the activity of this organization
    B. the community organization is attempting to widen the base of participation in all community affairs
    C. the agency is uncertain as to what the community wants
    D. the agency is uncertain as to what the community wants

8. Of the following, the LEAST likely way in which a records system may serve a supervisor is in   8._____
    A. developing a sympathetic and cooperative public attitude toward the agency
    B. improving the quality of supervision by permitting a check on the accomplishment of subordinates
    C. permit a precise prediction of the exact incidences in specific categories for the following year
    D. helping to take the guesswork out of the distribution of the agency

9. Assuming that the *grapevine* in any organization is virtually indestructible, the one of the following which it is MOST important for management to understand is:
   A. What is being spread by means of the *grapevine* and the reason for spreading it
   B. What is being spread by means of the *grapevine* and how it is being spread
   C. Who is involved in spreading the information that is on the *grapevine*
   D. Why those who are involved in spreading the information are doing so

9.____

10. When the supervisor writes a report concerning an investigation to which he has been assigned, it should be LEAST intended to provide
    A. a permanent official record of relevant information gathered
    B. a summary of case findings limited to facts which tend to indicate the guilt of a suspect
    C. a statement of the facts on which higher authorities may base a corrective or disciplinary action
    D. other investigators with information so that they may continue with other phases of the investigation

10.____

11. In survey work, questionnaires rather than interviews are sometimes used. The one of the following which is a DISADVANTAGE of the questionnaire method as compared with the interview is the
    A. difficulty of accurately interpreting the results
    B. problem of maintaining anonymity of the participant
    C. fact that it is relatively uneconomical
    D. requirement of special training for the distribution of questionnaires

11.____

12. in his contacts with the public, an employee should attempt to create a good climate of support for his agency.
    This statement is GENERALLY
    A. *false*; such attempts are clearly beyond the scope of his responsibility
    B. *true*; employees of an agency who come in contact with the public have the opportunity to affect public relations
    C. *false*; such activity should be restricted to supervisors trained in public relations techniques
    D. *true*; the future expansion of the agency depends to a great extent on continued public support of the agency

12.____

13. The repeated use by a supervisor of a call for volunteers to get a job done is objectionable MAINLY because it
    A. may create a feeling of animosity between the volunteers and the non-volunteers
    B. may indicate that the supervisor is avoiding responsibility for making assignments which will be most productive
    C. is an indication that the supervisor is not familiar with the individual capabilities of his men
    D. is unfair to men who, for valid reasons, do not, or cannot volunteer

13.____

14. Of the following statements concerning subordinates' expressions to a supervisor of their opinions and feelings concerning work situations, the one which is MOST correct is that
    A. by listening and responding to such expressions the supervisor encourages the development of complaints
    B. the lack of such expressions should indicate to the supervisor that there is a high level of job satisfaction
    C. the more the supervisor listens to and responds to such expressions, the more he demonstrates lack of supervisory ability
    D. by listening and responding to such expressions, the supervisor will enable many subordinates to understand and solve their own problems on the job

14._____

15. In attempting to motivate employees, rewards are considered preferable to punishment PRIMARILY because
    A. punishment seldom has any effect on human behavior
    B. punishment usually results in decreased production
    C. supervisors find it difficult to punish
    D. rewards are more likely to result in willing cooperation

15._____

16. In an attempt to combat the low morale in his organization, a high level supervisor publicized an *open-door policy* to allow employees who wished to do so to come to him with their complaints.
    Which of the following is LEAST likely to account for the fact that no employee came in with a complaint?
    A. Employees are generally reluctant to go over the heads of their immediate supervisor.
    B. The employees did not feel that management would help them.
    C. The low morale was not due to complaints associated with the job.
    D. The employees felt that they had more to lose than to gain.

16._____

17. It is MOST desirable to use written instructions rather than oral instructions for a particular job when
    A. a mistake on the job will not be serious
    B. the job can be completed in a short time
    C. there is no need to explain the job minutely
    D. the job involves many details

17._____

18. If you receive a telephone call regarding a matter which your office does not handle, you should FIRST
    A. give the caller the telephone number of the proper office so that he can dial again
    B. offer to transfer the caller to the proper office
    C. suggest that the caller re-dial since he probably dialed incorrectly
    D. tell the caller he has reached the wrong office and then hang up

18._____

19. When you answer the telephone, the MOST important reason for identifying yourself and your organization is to   19.____
    A. give the caller time to collect his or her thoughts
    B. impress the caller with your courtesy
    C. inform the caller that he or she has reached the right number
    D. set a business-like tone at the beginning of the conversation

20. As soon as you pick up the phone, a very angry caller begins immediately to complain about city agencies and *red tape*. He says that he has been shifted to two or three different offices. It turs out that he is seeking information which is not immediately available to you. You believe, you know, however, where it can be found.   20.____
Which of the following actions is the BEST one for you to take?
    A. To eliminate all confusion, suggest that the caller write the agency stating explicitly what he wants.
    B. Apologize by telling the caller how busy city agencies now are, but also tell him directly that you do not have the information he needs.
    C. Ask for the caller's telephone number and assure him you will call back after you have checked further.
    D. Give the caller the name and telephone number of the person who might be able to help, but explain that you are not positive he will get results/

21. Which of the following approaches usually provides the BEST communication in the objectives and values of a new program which is to be introduced?   21.____
    A. A general written description of the program by the program manager for review by those who share responsibility
    B. An effective verbal presentation by the program manager to those affected
    C. Development of the plan and operational approach in carrying out the program by the program manager assisted by his key subordinates
    D. Development of the plan by the program manager's supervisor

22. What is the BEST approach for introducing change?   22.____
A
    A. combination of written and also verbal communication to all personnel affected by the change
    B. general bulletin to all personnel
    C. meeting pointing out all the values of the new approach
    D. written directive to key personnel

23. Of the following, committees are BEST used for   23.____
    A. advising the head of the organization
    B. improving functional work
    C. making executive decisions
    D. making specific planning decisions

24. An effective discussion leader is one who   24.____
    A. announces the problem and his preconceived solution at the start of the
       discussion
    B. guides and directs the discussion according to pre-arranged outline
    C. interrupts or corrects confused participants to save time
    D. permits anyone to say anything at any time

25. The human relations movement in management theory is basically concerned   25.____
    with
    A. counteracting employee unrest
    B. eliminating the *time and motion* man
    C. interrelationships among individuals in organizations
    D. the psychology of the worker

_____

KEY (CORRECT ANSWERS)

1.	C		11.	A
2.	C		12.	B
3.	A		13.	B
4.	D		14.	D
5.	D		15.	D
6.	B		16.	C
7.	A		17.	D
8.	C		18.	B
9.	A		19.	C
10.	B		20.	C

21.	C
22.	A
23.	A
24.	B
25.	C

_____

PHILOSOPHY, PRINCIPLES, PRACTICES AND TECHNICS
OF
SUPERVISION, ADMINISTRATION, MANAGEMENT AND ORGANIZATION

TABLE OF CONTENTS

PHILOSOPHY, PRINCIPLES, PRACTICES, AND TECHNICS
OF
SUPERVISION, ADMINISTRATION, MANAGEMENT AND ORGANIZATION

I. MEANING OF SUPERVISION

The extension of the democratic philosophy has been accompanied by an extension in the scope of supervision. Modern leaders and supervisors no longer think of supervision in the narrow sense of being confined chiefly to visiting employees, supplying materials, or rating the staff. They regard supervision as being intimately related to all the concerned agencies of society, they speak of the supervisor's function in terms of "growth", rather than the "improvement," of employees.

This modern concept of supervision may be defined as follows:

Supervision is leadership and the development of leadership within groups which are cooperatively engaged in inspection, research, training, guidance and evaluation.

II. THE OLD AND THE NEW SUPERVISION

TRADITIONAL
1. Inspection
2. Focused on the employee
3. Visitation
4. Random and haphazard
5. Imposed and authoritarian
6. One person usually

MODERN
1. Study and analysis
2. Focused on aims, materials, methods, supervisors, employees, environment
3. Demonstrations, intervisitation, workshops, directed reading, bulletins, etc.
4. Definitely organized and planned (scientific)
5. Cooperative and democratic
6. Many persons involved (creative)

III THE EIGHT (8) BASIC PRINCIPLES OF THE NEW SUPERVISION

1. PRINCIPLE OF RESPONSIBILITY
Authority to act and responsibility for acting must be joined.
   a. If you give responsibility, give authority.
   b. Define employee duties clearly.
   c. Protect employees from criticism by others.
   d. Recognize the rights as well as obligations of employees.
   e. Achieve the aims of a democratic society insofar as it is possible within the area of your work.
   f. Establish a situation favorable to training and learning.
   g. Accept ultimate responsibility for everything done in your section, unit, office, division, department.
   h. Good administration and good supervision are inseparable.

2. *PRINCIPLE OF AUTHORITY*

The success of the supervisor is measured by the extent to which the power of authority is not used.

   a. Exercise simplicity and informality in supervision.
   b. Use the simplest machinery of supervision.
   c. If it is good for the organization as a whole, it is probably justified.
   d. Seldom be arbitrary or authoritative.
   e. Do not base your work on the power of position or of personality.
   f. Permit and encourage the free expression of opinions.

3. *PRINCIPLE OF SELF-GROWTH*

The success of the supervisor is measured by the extent to which, and the speed with which, he is no longer needed.

   a. Base criticism on principles, not on specifics.
   b. Point out higher activities to employees.
   c. Train for self-thinking by employees, to meet new situations.
   d. Stimulate initiative, self-reliance and individual responsibility.
   e. Concentrate on stimulating the growth of employees rather than on removing defects.

4. *PRINCIPLE OF INDIVIDUAL WORTH*

Respect for the individual is a paramount consideration in supervision.

   a. Be human and sympathetic in dealing with employees.
   b. Don't nag about things to be done.
   c. Recognize the individual differences among employees and seek opportunities to permit best expression of each personality.

5. *PRINCIPLE OF CREATIVE LEADERSHIP*

The best supervision is that which is not apparent to the employee.

   a. Stimulate, don't drive employees to creative action.
   b. Emphasize doing good things.
   c. Encourage employees to do what they do best.
   d. Do not be too greatly concerned with details of subject or method.
   e. Do not be concerned exclusively with immediate problems and activities.
   f. Reveal higher activities and make them both desired and maximally possible.
   g. Determine procedures in the light of each situation but see that these are derived from a sound basic philosophy.
   h. Aid, inspire and lead so as to liberate the creative spirit latent in all good employees.

6. *PRINCIPLE OF SUCCESS AND FAILURE*

There are no unsuccessful employees, only unsuccessful supervisors who have failed to give proper leadership.

   a. Adapt suggestions to the capacities, attitudes, and prejudices of employees.
   b. Be gradual, be progressive, be persistent.
   c. Help the employee find the general principle; have the employee apply his own problem to the general principle.
   d. Give adequate appreciation for good work and honest effort.
   e. Anticipate employee difficulties and help to prevent them.
   f. Encourage employees to do the desirable things they will do anyway.
   g. Judge your supervision by the results it secures.

7. *PRINCIPLE OF SCIENCE*

Successful supervision is scientific, objective, and experimental. It is based on facts, not on prejudices.

a. Be cumulative in results.
b. Never divorce your suggestions from the goals of training.
c. Don't be impatient of results.
d. Keep all matters on a professional, not a personal level.
e. Do not be concerned exclusively with immediate problems and activities.
f. Use objective means of determining achievement and rating where possible.

8. *PRINCIPLE OF COOPERATION*

Supervision is a cooperative enterprise between supervisor and employee.

a. Begin with conditions as they are.
b. Ask opinions of all involved when formulating policies.
c. Organization is as good as its weakest link.
d. Let employees help to determine policies and department programs.
e. Be approachable and accessible - physically and mentally.
f. Develop pleasant social relationships.

IV. WHAT IS ADMINISTRATION?

Administration is concerned with providing the environment, the material facilities, and the operational procedures that will promote the maximum growth and development of supervisors and employees. (Organization is an aspect, and a concomitant, of administration.)

There is no sharp line of demarcation between supervision and administration; these functions are intimately interrelated and, often, overlapping. They are complementary activities.

1. *PRACTICES COMMONLY CLASSED AS "SUPERVISORY"*

a. Conducting employees conferences
b. Visiting sections, units, offices, divisions, departments
c. Arranging for demonstrations
d. Examining plans
e. Suggesting professional reading
f. Interpreting bulletins
g. Recommending in-service training courses
h. Encouraging experimentation
i. Appraising employee morale
j. Providing for intervisitation

2. *PRACTICES COMMONLY CLASSIFIED AS "ADMINISTRATIVE"*

a. Management of the office
b. Arrangement of schedules for extra duties
c. Assignment of rooms or areas
d. Distribution of supplies
e. Keeping records and reports
f. Care of audio-visual materials
g. Keeping inventory records
h. Checking record cards and books
i. Programming special activities
j. Checking on the attendance and punctuality of employees

3. *PRACTICES COMMONLY CLASSIFIED AS BOTH "SUPERVISORY" AND "ADMINISTRATIVE"*
   a. Program construction
   b. Testing or evaluating outcomes
   c. Personnel accounting
   d. Ordering instructional materials

V. RESPONSIBILITIES OF THE SUPERVISOR

A person employed in a supervisory capacity must constantly be able to improve his own efficiency and ability. He represents the employer to the employees and only continuous self-examination can make him a capable supervisor.

Leadership and training are the supervisor's responsibility. An efficient working unit is one in which the employees work with the supervisor. It is his job to bring out the best in his employees. He must always be relaxed, courteous and calm in his association with his employees. Their feelings are important, and a harsh attitude does not develop the most efficient employees.

VI. COMPETENCIES OF THE SUPERVISOR

1. Complete knowledge of the duties and responsibilities of his position.
2. To be able to organize a job, plan ahead and carry through.
3. To have self-confidence and initiative.
4. To be able to handle the unexpected situation and make quick decisions.
5. To be able to properly train subordinates in the positions they are best suited for.
6. To be able to keep good human relations among his subordinates.
7. To be able to keep good human relations between his subordinates and himself and to earn their respect and trust.

VII. THE PROFESSIONAL SUPERVISOR-EMPLOYEE RELATIONSHIP

There are two kinds of efficiency: one kind is only apparent and is produced in organizations through the exercise of mere discipline; this is but a simulation of the second, or true, efficiency which springs from spontaneous cooperation. If you are a manager, no matter how great or small your responsibility, it is your job, in the final analysis, to create and develop this involuntary cooperation among the people whom you supervise. For, no matter how powerful a combination of money, machines, and materials a company may have, this is a dead and sterile thing without a team of willing, thinking and articulate people to guide it.

The following 21 points are presented as indicative of the exemplary basic relationship that should exist between supervisor and employee:

1. Each person wants to be liked and respected by his fellow employee and wants to be treated with consideration and respect by his superior.
2. The most competent employee will make an error. However, in a unit where good relations exist between the supervisor and his employees, tenseness and fear do not exist. Thus, errors are not hidden or covered up and the efficiency of a unit is not impaired.
3. Subordinates resent rules, regulations, or orders that are unreasonable or unexplained.
4. Subordinates are quick to resent unfairness, harshness, injustices and favoritism.
5. An employee will accept responsibility if he knows that he will be complimented for a job well done, and not too harshly chastised for failure; that his supervisor will check the cause of the failure, and, if it was the supervisor's fault, he will assume the blame therefore. If it was the employee's fault, his supervisor will explain the correct method or means of handling the responsibility.

6. An employee wants to receive credit for a suggestion he has made, that is used. If a suggestion cannot be used, the employee is entitled to an explanation. The supervisor should not say "no" and close the subject.
7. Fear and worry slow up a worker's ability. Poor working environment can impair his physical and mental health. A good supervisor avoids forceful methods, threats and arguments to get a job done.
8. A forceful supervisor is able to train his employees individually and as a team, and is able to motivate them in the proper channels.
9. A mature supervisor is able to properly evaluate his subordinates and to keep them happy and satisfied.
10. A sensitive supervisor will never patronize his subordinates.
11. A worthy supervisor will respect his employees' confidences.
12. Definite and clear-cut responsibilities should be assigned to each executive.
13. Responsibility should always be coupled with corresponding authority.
14. No change should be made in the scope or responsibilities of a position without a definite understanding to that effect on the part of all persons concerned.
15. No executive or employee, occupying a single position in the organization, should be subject to definite orders from more than one source.
16. Orders should never be given to subordinates over the head of a responsible executive. Rather than do this, the officer in question should be supplanted.
17. Criticisms of subordinates should, whoever possible, be made privately, and in no case should a subordinate be criticized in the presence of executives or employees of equal or lower rank.
18. No dispute or difference between executives or employees as to authority or responsibilities should be considered too trivial for prompt and careful adjudication.
19. Promotions, wage changes, and disciplinary action should always be approved by the executive immediately superior to the one directly responsible.
20. No executive or employee should ever be required, or expected, to be at the same time an assistant to, and critic of, another.
21. Any executive whose work is subject to regular inspection should, whever practicable, be given the assistance and facilities necessary to enable him to maintain an independent check of the quality of his work.

VIII. MINI-TEXT IN SUPERVISION, ADMINISTRATION, MANAGEMENT, AND ORGANIZATION

A. BRIEF HIGHLIGHTS

Listed concisely and sequentially are major headings and important data in the field for quick recall and review.

1. *LEVELS OF MANAGEMENT*
Any organization of some size has several levels of management. In terms of a ladder the levels are:

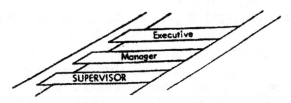

The first level is very important because it is the beginning point of management leadership.

2. WHAT THE SUPERVISOR MUST LEARN
A supervisor must learn to:
(1) Deal with people and their differences
(2) Get the job done through people
(3) Recognize the problems when they exist
(4) Overcome obstacles to good performance
(5) Evaluate the performance of people
(6) Check his own performance in terms of accomplishment

3. A DEFINITION OF SUPERVISOR
The term supervisor means any individual having authority, in the interests of the employer, to hire, transfer, suspend, lay-off, recall, promote, discharge, assign, reward, or discipline other employees or responsibility to direct them, or to adjust their grievances, or effectively to recommend such action, if, in connection with the foregoing, exercise of such authority is not of a merely routine or clerical nature but requires the use of independent judgment.

4. ELEMENTS OF THE TEAM CONCEPT
What is involved in teamwork? The component parts are:
(1) Members	(3) Goals	(5) Cooperation
(2) A leader	(4) Plans	(6) Spirit

5. PRINCIPLES OF ORGANIZATION
(1) A team member must know what his job is.
(2) Be sure that the nature and scope of a job are understood.
(3) Authority and responsibility should be carefully spelled out.
(4) A supervisor should be permitted to make the maximum number of decisions affecting his employees.
(5) Employees should report to only one supervisor.
(6) A supervisor should direct only as many employees as he can handle effectively.
(7) An organization plan should be flexible.
(8) Inspection and performance of work should be separate.
(9) Organizational problems should receive immediate attention.
(10) Assign work in line with ability and experience.

6. THE FOUR IMPORTANT PARTS OF EVERY JOB
(1) Inherent in every job is the *accountability* for results.
(2) A second set of factors in every job is *responsibilities.*
(3) Along with duties and responsibilities one must have the *authority* to act within certain limits without obtaining permission to proceed.
(4) No job exists in a vacuum. The supervisor is surrounded by key *relationships.*

7. PRINCIPLES OF DELEGATION
Where work is delegated for the first time, the supervisor should think in terms of these questions:
(1) Who is best qualified to do this?
(2) Can an employee improve his abilities by doing this?
(3) How long should an employee spend on this?
(4) Are there any special problems for which he will need guidance?
(5) How broad a delegation can I make?

8. PRINCIPLES OF EFFECTIVE COMMUNICATIONS
(1) Determine the media
(2) To whom directed?
(3) Identification and source authority
(4) Is communication understood?

9. PRINCIPLES OF WORK IMPROVEMENT
(1) Most people usually do only the work which is assigned to them
(2) Workers are likely to fit assigned work into the time available to perform it
(3) A good workload usually stimulates output
(4) People usually do their best work when they know that results will be reviewed or inspected
(5) Employees usually feel that someone else is responsible for conditions of work, workplace layout, job methods, type of tools/equipment, and other such factors
(6) Employees are usually defensive about their job security
(7) Employees have natural resistance to change
(8) Employees can support or destroy a supervisor
(9) A supervisor usually earns the respect of his people through his personal example of diligence and efficiency

10. AREAS OF JOB IMPROVEMENT
The areas of job improvement are quite numerous, but the most common ones which a supervisor can identify and utilize are:

(1) Departmental layout
(2) Flow of work
(3) Workplace layout
(4) Utilization of manpower
(5) Work methods
(6) Materials handling
(7) Utilization
(8) Motion economy

11. SEVEN KEY POINTS IN MAKING IMPROVEMENTS
(1) Select the job to be improved
(2) Study how it is being done now
(3) Question the present method
(4) Determine actions to be taken
(5) Chart proposed method
(6) Get approval and apply
(7) Solicit worker participation

12. CORRECTIVE TECHNIQUES OF JOB IMPROVEMENT

Specific Problems	General Improvement	Corrective Techniques
(1) Size of workload	(1) Departmental layout	(1) Study with scale model
(2) Inability to meet schedules	(2) Flow of work	(2) Flow chart study
(3) Strain and fatigue	(3) Work plan layout	(3) Motion analysis
(4) Improper use of men and skills	(4) Utilization of manpower	(4) Comparison of units produced to standard allowance
(5) Waste, poor quality, unsafe conditions	(5) Work methods	(5) Methods analysis
(6) Bottleneck conditions that hinder output	(6) Materials handling	(6) Flow chart & equipment study
(7) Poor utilization of equipment and machine	(7) Utilization of equipment	(7) Down time vs. running time
(8) Efficiency and productivity of labor	(8) Motion economy	(8) Motion analysis

127

13. A PLANNING CHECKLIST
(1) Objectives
(2) Controls
(3) Delegations
(4) Communications
(5) Resources

(6) Resources
(7) Manpower
(8) Equipment
(9) Supplies and materials
(10) Utilization of time

(11) Safety
(12) Money
(13) Work
(14) Timing of improvements

14. FIVE CHARACTERISTICS OF GOOD DIRECTIONS
In order to get results, directions must be:
(1) Possible of accomplishment
(2) Agreeable with worker interests
(3) Related to mission
(4) Planned and complete
(5) Unmistakably clear

15. TYPES OF DIRECTIONS
(1) Demands or direct orders
(2) Requests
(3) Suggestion or implication
(4) Volunteering

16. CONTROLS
A typical listing of the overall areas in which the supervisor should establish controls might be:
(1) Manpower
(2) Materials
(3) Quality of work
(4) Quantity of work
(5) Time
(6) Space
(7) Money
(8) Methods

17. ORIENTING THE NEW EMPLOYEE
(1) Prepare for him
(2) Welcome the new employee
(3) Orientation for the job
(4) Follow-up

18. CHECKLIST FOR ORIENTING NEW EMPLOYEES

Yes   No

(1) Do your appreciate the feelings of new employees when they first report for work?

(2) Are you aware of the fact that the new employee must make a big adjustment to his job?

(3) Have you given him good reasons for liking the job and the organization?

(4) Have you prepared for his first day on the job?

(5) Did you welcome him cordially and make him feel needed?

(6) Did you establish rapport with him so that he feels free to talk and discuss matters with you?

(7) Did you explain his job to him and his relationship to you?

(8) Does he know that his work will be evaluated periodically on a basis that is fair and objective?

(9) Did you introduce him to his fellow workers in such a way that they are likely to accept him?

(10) Does he know what employee benefits he will receive?

(11) Does he understand the importance of being on the job and what to do if he must leave his duty station?

(12) Has he been impressed with the importance of accident prevention and safe practice?

(13) Does he generally know his way around the department?

(14) Is he under the guidance of a sponsor who will teach the right ways of doing things?

(15) Do you plan to follow-up so that he will continue to adjust successfully to his job?

19. *PRINCIPLES OF LEARNING*
(1) Motivation   (2) Demonstration or explanation   (3) Practice

20. *CAUSES OF POOR PERFORMANCE*
(1) Improper training for job
(2) Wrong tools
(3) Inadequate directions
(4) Lack of supervisory follow-up
(5) Poor communications
(6) Lack of standards of performance
(7) Wrong work habits
(8) Low morale
(9) Other

21. *FOUR MAJOR STEPS IN ON-THE-JOB INSTRUCTION*
(1) Prepare the worker
(2) Present the operation
(3) Tryout performance
(4) Follow-up

22. *EMPLOYEES WANT FIVE THINGS*
(1) Security (2) Opportunity (3) Recognition (4) Inclusion (5) Expression

23. *SOME DON'TS IN REGARD TO PRAISE*
(1) Don't praise a person for something he hasn't done
(2) Don't praise a person unless you can be sincere
(3) Don't be sparing in praise just because your superior withholds it from you
(4) Don't let too much time elapse between good performance and recognition of it

24. *HOW TO GAIN YOUR WORKERS' CONFIDENCE*
Methods of developing confidence include such things as:
(1) Knowing the interests, habits, hobbies of employees
(2) Admitting your own inadequacies
(3) Sharing and telling of confidence in others
(4) Supporting people when they are in trouble
(5) Delegating matters that can be well handled
(6) Being frank and straightforward about problems and working conditions
(7) Encouraging others to bring their problems to you
(8) Taking action on problems which impede worker progress

25. *SOURCES OF EMPLOYEE PROBLEMS*
On-the-job causes might be such things as:
(1) A feeling that favoritism is exercised in assignments
(2) Assignment of overtime
(3) An undue amount of supervision
(4) Changing methods or systems
(5) Stealing of ideas or trade secrets
(6) Lack of interest in job
(7) Threat of reduction in force
(8) Ignorance or lack of communications
(9) Poor equipment
(10) Lack of knowing how supervisor feels toward employee
(11) Shift assignments

Off-the-job problems might have to do with:
(1) Health   (2) Finances   (3) Housing   (4) Family

26. *THE SUPERVISOR'S KEY TO DISCIPLINE*

There are several key points about discipline which the supervisor should keep in mind:

    (1) Job discipline is one of the disciplines of life and is directed by the supervisor.
    (2) It is more important to correct an employee fault than to fix blame for it.
    (3) Employee performance is affected by problems both on the job and off.
    (4) Sudden or abrupt changes in behavior can be indications of important employee problems.
    (5) Problems should be dealt with as soon as possible after they are identified.
    (6) The attitude of the supervisor may have more to do with solving problems than the techniques of problem solving.
    (7) Correction of employee behavior should be resorted to only after the supervisor is sure that training or counseling will not be helpful.
    (8) Be sure to document your disciplinary actions.
    (9) Make sure that you are disciplining on the basis of facts rather than personal feelings.
    (10) Take each disciplinary step in order, being careful not to make snap judgments, or decisions based on impatience.

27. *FIVE IMPORTANT PROCESSES OF MANAGEMENT*

    (1) Planning   (2) Organizing   (3) Scheduling
    (4) Controlling   (5) Motivating

28. *WHEN THE SUPERVISOR FAILS TO PLAN*

    (1) Supervisor creates impression of not knowing his job
    (2) May lead to excessive overtime
    (3) Job runs itself -- supervisor lacks control
    (4) Deadlines and appointments missed
    (5) Parts of the work go undone
    (6) Work interrupted by emergencies
    (7) Sets a bad example
    (8) Uneven workload creates peaks and valleys
    (9) Too much time on minor details at expense of more important tasks

29. *FOURTEEN GENERAL PRINCIPLES OF MANAGEMENT*

    (1) Division of work
    (2) Authority and responsibility
    (3) Discipline
    (4) Unity of command
    (5) Unity of direction
    (6) Subordination of individual interest to general interest
    (7) Remuneration of personnel
    (8) Centralization
    (9) Scalar chain
    (10) Order
    (11) Equity
    (12) Stability of tenure of personnel
    (13) Initiative
    (14) Esprit de corps

30. *CHANGE*

Bringing about change is perhaps attempted more often, and yet less well understood, than anything else the supervisor does. How do people generally react to change? (People tend to resist change that is imposed upon them by other individuals or circumstances.

Change is characteristic of every situation. It is a part of every real endeavor where the efforts of people are concerned.

A. Why do people resist change?
   People may resist change because of:
   (1) Fear of the unknown
   (2) Implied criticism
   (3) Unpleasant experiences in the past
   (4) Fear of loss of status
   (5) Threat to the ego
   (6) Fear of loss of economic stability

B. How can we best overcome the resistance to change?
   In initiating change, take these steps:
   (1) Get ready to sell
   (2) Identify sources of help
   (3) Anticipate objections
   (4) Sell benefits
   (5) Listen in depth
   (6) Follow up

B. BRIEF TOPICAL SUMMARIES

I. WHO/WHAT IS THE SUPERVISOR?
1. The supervisor is often called the "highest level employee and the lowest level manager."
2. A supervisor is a member of both management and the work group. He acts as a bridge between the two.
3. Most problems in supervision are in the area of human relations, or people problems.
4. Employees expect: Respect, opportunity to learn and to advance, and a sense of belonging, and so forth.
5. Supervisors are responsible for directing people and organizing work. Planning is of paramount importance.
6. A position description is a set of duties and responsibilities inherent to a given position.
7. It is important to keep the position description up-to-date and to provide each employee with his own copy.

II. THE SOCIOLOGY OF WORK
1. People are alike in many ways; however, each individual is unique.
2. The supervisor is challenged in getting to know employee differences. Acquiring skills in evaluating individuals is an asset.
3. Maintaining meaningful working relationships in the organization is of great importance.
4. The supervisor has an obligation to help individuals to develop to their fullest potential.
5. Job rotation on a planned basis helps to build versatility and to maintain interest and enthusiasm in work groups.
6. Cross training (job rotation) provides backup skills.
7. The supervisor can help reduce tension by maintaining a sense of humor, providing guidance to employees, and by making reasonable and timely decisions. Employees respond favorably to working under reasonably predictable circumstances.
8. Change is characteristic of all managerial behavior. The supervisor must adjust to changes in procedures, new methods, technological changes, and to a number of new and sometimes challenging situations.
9. To overcome the natural tendency for people to resist change, the supervisor should become more skillful in initiating change.

III. PRINCIPLES AND PRACTICES OF SUPERVISION

1. Employees should be required to answer to only one superior.
2. A supervisor can effectively direct only a limited number of employees, depending upon the complexity, variety, and proximity of the jobs involved.
3. The organizational chart presents the organization in graphic form. It reflects lines of authority and responsibility as well as interrelationships of units within the organization.
4. Distribution of work can be improved through an analysis using the "Work Distribution Chart."
5. The "Work Distribution Chart" reflects the division of work within a unit in understandable form.
6. When related tasks are given to an employee, he has a better chance of increasing his skills through training.
7. The individual who is given the responsibility for tasks must also be given the appropriate authority to insure adequate results.
8. The supervisor should delegate repetitive, routine work. Preparation of recurring reports, maintaining leave and attendance records are some examples.
9. Good discipline is essential to good task performance. Discipline is reflected in the actions of employees on the job in the absence of supervision.
10. Disciplinary action may have to be taken when the positive aspects of discipline have failed. Reprimand, warning, and suspension are examples of disciplinary action.
11. If a situation calls for a reprimand, be sure it is deserved and remember it is to be done in private.

IV. DYNAMIC LEADERSHIP

1. A style is a personal method or manner of exerting influence.
2. Authoritarian leaders often see themselves as the source of power and authority.
3. The democratic leader often perceives the group as the source of authority and power.
4. Supervisors tend to do better when using the pattern of leadership that is most natural for them.
5. Social scientists suggest that the effective supervisor use the leadership style that best fits the problem or circumstances involved.
6. All four styles -- telling, selling, consulting, joining -- have their place. Using one does not preclude using the other at another time.
7. The theory X point of view assumes that the average person dislikes work, will avoid it whenever possible, and must be coerced to achieve organizational objectives.
8. The theory Y point of view assumes that the average person considers work to be as natural as play, and, when the individual is committed, he requires little supervision or direction to accomplish desired objectives.
9. The leader's basic assumptions concerning human behavior and human nature affect his actions, decisions, and other managerial practices.
10. Dissatisfaction among employees is often present, but difficult to isolate. The supervisor should seek to weaken dissatisfaction by keeping promises, being sincere and considerate, keeping employees informed, and so forth.
11. Constructive suggestions should be encouraged during the natural progress of the work.

V. PROCESSES FOR SOLVING PROBLEMS

1. People find their daily tasks more meaningful and satisfying when they can improve them.
2. The causes of problems, or the key factors, are often hidden in the background. Ability to solve problems often involves the ability to isolate them from their backgrounds. There is some substance to the cliché that some persons "can't see the forest for the trees."
3. New procedures are often developed from old ones. Problems should be broken down into manageable parts. New ideas can be adapted from old ones.

4. People think differently in problem-solving situations. Using a logical, patterned approach is often useful. One approach found to be useful includes these steps:

    (a) Define the problem   (d) Weigh and decide
    (b) Establish objectives   (e) Take action
    (c) Get the facts   (f) Evaluate action

VI. TRAINING FOR RESULTS

1. Participants respond best when they feel training is important to them.
2. The supervisor has responsibility for the training and development of those who report to him.
3. When training is delegated to others, great care must be exercised to insure the trainer has knowledge, aptitude, and interest for his work as a trainer.
4. Training (learning) of some type goes on continually. The most successful supervisor makes certain the learning contributes in a productive manner to operational goals.
5. New employees are particularly susceptible to training. Older employees facing new job situations require specific training, as well as having need for development and growth opportunities.
6. Training needs require continuous monitoring.
7. The training officer of an agency is a professional with a responsibility to assist supervisors in solving training problems.
8. Many of the self-development steps important to the supervisor's own growth are equally important to the development of peers and subordinates. Knowledge of these is important when the supervisor consults with others on development and growth opportunities.

VII. HEALTH, SAFETY, AND ACCIDENT PREVENTION

1. Management-minded supervisors take appropriate measures to assist employees in maintaining health and in assuring safe practices in the work environment.
2. Effective safety training and practices help to avoid injury and accidents.
3. Safety should be a management goal. All infractions of safety which are observed should be corrected without exception.
4. Employees' safety attitude, training and instruction, provision of safe tools and equipment, supervision, and leadership are considered highly important factors which contribute to safety and which can be influenced directly by supervisors.
5. When accidents do occur they should be investigated promptly for very important reasons, including the fact that information which is gained can be used to prevent accidents in the future.

VIII. EQUAL EMPLOYMENT OPPORTUNITY

1. The supervisor should endeavor to treat all employees fairly, without regard to religion, race, sex, or national origin.
2. Groups tend to reflect the attitude of the leader. Prejudice can be detected even in very subtle form. Supervisors must strive to create a feeling of mutual respect and confidence in every employee.
3. Complete utilization of all human resources is a national goal. Equitable consideration should be accorded women in the work force, minority-group members, the physically and mentally handicapped, and the older employee. The important question is: "Who can do the job?"
4. Training opportunities, recognition for performance, overtime assignments, promotional opportunities, and all other personnel actions are to be handled on an equitable basis.

IX. IMPROVING COMMUNICATIONS

1. Communications is achieving understanding between the sender and the receiver of a message. It also means sharing information -- the creation of understanding.
2. Communication is basic to all human activity. Words are means of conveying meanings; however, real meanings are in people.
3. There are very practical differences in the effectiveness of one-way, impersonal, and two-way communications. Words spoken face-to-face are better understood. Telephone conversations are effective, but lack the rapport of person-to-person exchanges. The whole person communicates.
4. Cooperation and communication in an organization go hand in hand. When there is a mutual respect between people, spelling out rules and procedures for communicating is unnecessary.
5. There are several barriers to effective communications. These include failure to listen with respect and understanding, lack of skill in feedback, and misinterpreting the meanings of words used by the speaker. It is also common practice to listen to what we want to hear, and tune out things we do not want to hear.
6. Communication is management's chief problem. The supervisor should accept the challenge to communicate more effectively and to improve interagency and intra-agency communications.
7. The supervisor may often plan for and conduct meetings. The planning phase is critical and may determine the success or the failure of a meeting.
8. Speaking before groups usually requires extra effort. Stage fright may never disappear completely, but it can be controlled.

X. SELF-DEVELOPMENT

1. Every employee is responsible for his own self-development.
2. Toastmaster and toastmistress clubs offer opportunities to improve skills in oral communications.
3. Planning for one's own self-development is of vital importance. Supervisors know their own strengths and limitations better than anyone else.
4. Many opportunities are open to aid the supervisor in his developmental efforts, including job assignments; training opportunities, both governmental and non-governmental -- to include universities and professional conferences and seminars.
5. Programmed instruction offers a means of studying at one's own rate.
6. Where difficulties may arise from a supervisor's being away from his work for training, he may participate in televised home study or correspondence courses to meet his self-develop- ment needs.

XI. TEACHING AND TRAINING

A. The Teaching Process

Teaching is encouraging and guiding the learning activities of students toward established goals. In most cases this process consists in five steps: preparation, presentation, summarization, evaluation, and application.

1. Preparation

Preparation is twofold in nature; that of the supervisor and the employee.
Preparation by the supervisor is absolutely essential to success. He must know what, when, where, how, and whom he will teach. Some of the factors that should be considered are:

(1) The objectives
(2) The materials needed
(3) The methods to be used
(4) Employee participation
(5) Employee interest
(6) Training aids
(7) Evaluation
(8) Summarization

Employee preparation consists in preparing the employee to receive the material. Probably the most important single factor in the preparation of the employee is arousing and maintaining his interest. He must know the objectives of the training, why he is there, how the material can be used, and its importance to him.

2. Presentation

In presentation, have a carefully designed plan and follow it.
The plan should be accurate and complete, yet flexible enough to meet situations as they arise. The method of presentation will be determined by the particular situation and objectives.

3. Summary

A summary should be made at the end of every training unit and program. In addition, there may be internal summaries depending on the nature of the material being taught. The important thing is that the trainee must always be able to understand how each part of the new material relates to the whole.

4. Application

The supervisor must arrange work so the employee will be given a chance to apply new knowledge or skills while the material is still clear in his mind and interest is high. The trainee does not really know whether he has learned the material until he has been given a chance to apply it. If the material is not applied, it loses most of its value.

5. Evaluation

The purpose of all training is to promote learning. To determine whether the training has been a success or failure, the supervisor must evaluate this learning.
In the broadest sense evaluation includes all the devices, methods, skills, and techniques used by the supervisor to keep him self and the employees informed as to their progress toward the objectives they are pursuing. The extent to which the employee has mastered the knowledge, skills, and abilities, or changed his attitudes, as determined by the program objectives, is the extent to which instruction has succeeded or failed.
Evaluation should not be confined to the end of the lesson, day, or program but should be used continuously. We shall note later the way this relates to the rest of the teaching process.

B. Teaching Methods

A teaching method is a pattern of identifiable student and instructor activity used in presenting training material.
All supervisors are faced with the problem of deciding which method should be used at a given time.
As with all methods, there are certain advantages and disadvantages to each method.

1. Lecture

The lecture is direct oral presentation of material by the supervisor. The present trend is to place less emphasis on the trainer's activity and more on that of the trainee.

2. Discussion

Teaching by discussion or conference involves using questions and other techniques to arouse interest and focus attention upon certain areas, and by doing so creating a learning situation. This can be one of the most valuable methods because it gives the employees 'an opportunity to express their ideas and pool their knowledge.

3. Demonstration

The demonstration is used to teach how something works or how to do something. It can be used to show a principle or what the results of a series of actions will be. A well-staged demonstration is particularly effective because it shows proper methods of performance in a realistic manner.

4. Performance

Performance is one of the most fundamental of all learning techniques or teaching methods. The trainee may be able to tell how a specific operation should be performed but he cannot be sure he knows how to perform the operation until he has done so.

5. Which Method to Use

Moreover, there are other methods and techniques of teaching. It is difficult to use any method without other methods entering into it. In any learning situation a combination of methods is usually more effective than anyone method alone.

Finally, evaluation must be integrated into the other aspects of the teaching-learning process.
It must be used in the motivation of the trainees; it must be used to assist in developing understanding during the training; and it must be related to employee application of the results of training.
This is distinctly the role of the supervisor.